passionate embrace

passionate embrace

FAITH, FLESH, TANGO

Sandra Vander Schaaf

CLEMENTS PUBLISHING GROUP

TORONTO

Clements Publishing Group Inc.
6021 Yonge Street, Box 213
Toronto, Ontario M2M 3W2 Canada
www.clementspublishing.com

Artist's Notes:
This is a work of non-fiction. To protect the privacy of
those whose stories intersect my own, most names and
some identifying details have been changed. I have
occasionally omitted people and events, but only when
that omission had no impact on the veracity or substance
of the story. To the best of my ability, I have accurately
reconstructed events and dialogue, but acknowledge that
there will be inevitable errors.

The photos scattered among these pages are offered as an
invitation to engage visually with the themes of the book.
While these images do reflect elements of the tango
experience that are explored in *Passionate Embrace*, in no
case do they depict any specific scene described in the text.

A cataloguing record for this publication
is available from Library and Archives Canada.

ISBN 978-1-926798-33-2 (paper)
ISBN 978-1-926798-37-0 (electronic)

For Peter

Contents

Acknowledgements

I am deeply grateful to a great many people. A broad community of support helped bring this book into being.

Thank you, Nicola Aimé and Susan Pieters, for your writerly wisdom, faithful encouragement, hard questions, and quick laughter.

Thank you to the people of St. Paul's Anglican Church, for putting up with all those tango analogies during sermon talk-backs, and for embodying the challenge and joy of extending God's generous embrace to the world.

Thank you to the Vancouver Argentine Tango community, for introducing me to the beauty and mystery of this incredible dance, for teaching me, challenging me, for taking me into your arms and onto the dance floor.

Thank you to the folk who first saw the potential of this crazy story: Ali Cumming, Maxine Hancock, Duffy Lott Gibb, Cherith Nordling Fee, Dal Schindell, Loren Wilkinson.

Thank you, Dr. Gail Dodek Wenner, physician, artist, encourager.

Thank you to my father (of blessed memory) and my mother, for your love, support, and encouragement.

Above all, thank you, my beloved Peter, for all you've given to make this dream come true.

Prologue

I did not expect to find God in tango. When I set foot in the *Strictly Tango* studio to see it danced, live, for the first time, I was indulging curiosity. When I signed up for lessons, I was trying on a hobby for size. When I bought my first pair of stilettos, I was buying equipment for a recreational diversion. In all these beginning steps, it never occurred to me that tango lessons and stilettos would propel me onto a spiritual journey, that Argentine Tango would become for me a tangible, physical, sensual way of knowing myself, and knowing God.

It might have turned out much differently, of course, for a thousand reasons. I credit grace for giving me the heart to seek more, to see beyond fishnet stockings and other tango clichés. Grace is the name for what happens when the Divine dips a finger into the dull and dusty stuff of life and transforms it into riches beyond description. Under what other influence could the sweaty and awkward interactions of novice dancers be transformed into something akin to divine communion?

I might have gone through all the motions of a beginner dancer only to give it up after a couple of months. Many do. In the early stages of learning it's hard to endure long evenings on the sidelines, the dejection, and heading home at the end of the night without a single dance. But grace was plentiful, and I found my way past those wallflower nights, past the novice stumbling, into nights sweet with tango intimacy.

It might also have turned out differently if I had launched into tango with an eye only to the prospect of holding and being held, looking for skin deep comfort in pseudo-sexual encounters. It's not for nothing that they call tango "the vertical expression of horizontal desire." Instead, perhaps miraculously, I found something holy in tango's embrace.

In retrospect, I can trace the pattern of that finger in the dust, the action of grace that enriched my experience of tango beyond any reasonable expectation. Grace traced its finger on my skin, along the contours of my body, along sinews and synapses, until I could no longer deny that my body mattered to God. What a wonder to discover that I am the dust that Grace transformed.

I feel compelled to tell this story, just as I feel compelled to dance, in spite of my lack of skill and elegance. I tell it not because it's my story and you should have any interest in me, but because I believe it is everybody's story—every *body's* story—and there's too little in this world that speaks for the body. So with inadequate words and tentative steps, I'll try now to describe how tango seduced me into my own body, and danced me into the arms of God.

CHAPTER ONE

My first venture into the world of tango had all the ingredients of a blind date. A slight acquaintance, piqued curiosity, a mutual friend setting up the time and the place, the anticipation, anxiety over what to wear, butterflies in the stomach. I had no idea what to expect. I knew only that I would not dance on the first night. Certainly not. It would be a night of observation only. This would be my first *milonga*. The word itself tasted like a dance, its syllables tripping gently from my lips, to my tongue, to my throat. I double-checked the address I had scribbled on a scrap of paper before heading out: 505 Hamilton Street. My palms were sweating as I pulled open the door.

The music was the first to greet me—simultaneously melodious and melancholic, from another time and another place. I stepped over the threshold and found myself in a small, dark vestibule, crowded with coats and piles of shoes and umbrellas. It was a grown-up version of what I remembered of the entrance to my kindergarten classroom, pungent with the odour of wet coats and boots, almost empty lunch boxes, and the funky smelling things kindergarteners forget to bring home from school. There was something of the same stale dampness in the air, and something of the same nervous anticipation in my gut. I was uncertain of my place in this world. I felt small. A little bit scared. And excited.

I pressed my raincoat into the coat rack without the benefit of a hanger. There were no more hangers to be had and the coats were pressed so tightly that hangers were unnecessary. It was difficult to take a deep breath in the close, dark space. Moving forward, it felt as I suppose it felt for Lucy to step through the Wardrobe into Narnia, or for Alice to tumble down the rabbit hole. It was surreal, as if I were stepping into someone else's story.

My eyes adjusted to the dimness of the room and confirmed what the music had already intimated. I was in another place, another time. There were fourteen-foot ceilings, tall windows framed with lush wine-coloured curtains, and a fireplace glowing with orange light in the far corner of the hall. Simple metal chairs were lined up around the circumference of the room, draped with discarded sweaters, shawls and suit jackets. The ring of folding chairs was interrupted here and there by small tea tables littered with votive candles, wine glasses, eye glasses, and water bottles.

There was a warm thrum of conversation—above a whisper and below conversational tone—respectfully mingling with the music, a little louder by the impromptu bar in the corner opposite the fireplace. Conversation framed the room, but most of those chatting seemed to forego eye contact in favour of a steady focus on the dancers. Solitary observers sat quietly, with crossed legs swinging ever so slightly to the rhythm of the music, or with feet marking the time on the hardwood floor. Some sat perched on the edge of their seats, ready to take to the dance floor at the slightest invitation, like birds alert to flight.

Dancers filled the interior space of the room. Feet made gentle shushing sounds on the hardwood floor, a rhythmic shuffling creating an undercurrent for the music, a sound at once earthy and unearthly. Many of the women danced with eyes closed. The men danced with eyes open but were every bit as focused on the rhythms and the movement of the dance. There was a trance-like quality to their concentration. I saw curves and lines. I saw bodies propelled, restrained, released, dancing, dancing, dancing.

I was immediately satisfied that I had followed through on this particular blind date. Though typically an indication of a bad date, in this first encounter with tango I was prepared to let tango do all the talking. Eager to find a place to settle for a promising night of observation, I took a deep breath and forced my eyes past the dancers to scan for an empty chair. I plotted a careful course to the far side of the room and claimed an empty chair near the fireplace.

I cannot account for how quickly I felt comfortable here. Dim light, velvet curtains, the rhythmic shuffling of soft-soled shoes, the gentle murmur of conversation, women dancing with every sense but sight. And there was something about the music, something rich and soulful. It was gentle but insistent, filling the space like rain into parched soil. It was the musical equivalent of a quilt, one made of every lovely and every sad memory you've ever had, the sort of quilt you'd wrap yourself in to have a cry, the sort of cry you'd later call good.

I saw him enter the room through the same vestibule, smiling, greeting friends as he made his way toward the corner where I was sitting. He caught my eye, just a few steps into the room. He smiled at me. I smiled back. He then turned his attention to friendly greetings and handshakes. I know now what it meant to allow my eyes to meet his, and to smile. At the time I was just being polite. (Though I'll admit that my smile may have been strangely exaggerated. I was, after all, in the process of falling in love with tango.) What I did not know then was that by allowing my gaze to be arrested by his, and by returning his smile with my own, I had unwittingly agreed to dance. I had unwittingly participated in the longstanding tango tradition of *cabeceo*. This was my first, glorious, tango mistake.

The *cabeceo* says a lot about tango. It is a practice that takes the sting of public rejection entirely out of the dance experience. It's one of the things that makes tango gracious, graceful. It would have revolutionized high school dances for the painfully shy. Rejection is still a possibility in tango, but it does not trip into the realm of public humiliation. There's no nervous walk across the dance floor, no agonizing over finding just the right words, no tittering friends rolling their eyes at the ill-placed audacity of your proposition, no cruel rejection, no heartsick march of humiliation back to your side of the gym. Instead, an invitation is given and received with the eyes. From wherever you are in the room, you send your gaze toward the one you'd like to dance with and wait for eye contact. When eyes have met, you incline your head slightly with an inquisitive nod. If your desired dance partner looks away, there will be no dance. Only the two of you need know that there was ever an invitation issued. If, however, your desired dance partner holds your gaze and nods or smiles, you can be assured that when it comes to extending a visible, public invitation, the answer will be yes.

He continued along the sidelines of the room, with cheek-to-cheek kisses for the women, in the local fashion—a kiss to the left and a kiss to the right—and handshakes or nods for the men. He had the air of a regular and seemed to know everyone. I went back to watching the dancers, taking in the general splendour of the night. It surprised me therefore, to find him standing directly in front of me. He smiled and extended his hand to me in the most gentlemanly manner I had ever seen in real life. It was the sort of gesture one might expect of a prince, the sort of gesture generally accompanied with a bow. He might have bowed a little, actually, he was so gracious and courteous, and confident. Picture Prince Charming inviting Cinderella to rise, to test the fit of the glass slipper he'd just slipped upon her dainty foot. "Shall we dance?" he asked, with every expectation that my answer would be yes, since, apparently, I had already agreed to do so.

Lacking both glass slippers and the ability to dance, I stammered my excuses. "I don't know how to dance tango. This is my first milonga. I'm just here to watch."

"Can you walk?"

There was only one answer. "Yes."

"Then," he said, with his hand still extended, having never once wavered in the gesture of invitation, "We will walk."

Cinderella I'm not, but something quite magical happened just then. It's the closest I've ever come to feeling part of a fairy tale. I accepted his extended hand, got up from my seat, and found myself—entirely unexpectedly, and yet quite naturally—in his embrace.

All night, I told everyone who asked me the same thing, "This is my first milonga. I don't know how to tango. I'm just here to watch." But they kept asking and I kept walking, until the walking felt like dancing, and the dancing felt like falling in love.

A lifetime ago, a skinny young minister, with ears too big for his head and teeth too big for his smile, stood in front of his congregation. On this particular morning, he stood before them not as their pastor but as my father. Beside him stood his wife, my mother, a beautiful blonde who, on more than one occasion, had been told she was a ringer for Doris Day. I was their babe in arms, their beloved daughter, three-months old and with just enough hair on my head to declare that I would definitely be a redhead, though my mother preferred to call me a "strawberry blonde." I was dressed in a borrowed baptismal gown, lacy and white, with a long flowing skirt. My mother tells me I was a good baby and didn't cry during the service and there's no reason not to believe her.

There were songs, and prayers, two readings from the Word of God, and then the baptism. These young parents of mine passed me from their arms to those of a beloved and long time friend, the minister who had presided over both their wedding and the baptism of their firstborn, my brother. Holy words were spoken, promises were made, water was poured into the baptismal font and blessed. At the appropriate time, with the appropriate solemnity, I was shifted into a one-armed cradle hold so the baptizer could hold me over the font and still have a hand free for the blessing. The congregation held a collective breath—some in awe of the sacred rite, others quietly wondering if I was about to unceremoniously object to getting unexpectedly wet. Then, with fingers dipping into the waters and dripping over my head with each of the names of God, he said, "Sandra Alison Vander Schaaf, I baptize you in the name of the Father, the Son, and the Holy Spirit. Amen." The he traced the mark of a cross on my forehead with damp fingers, saying, "Sandra, child of the covenant in baptism, you are sealed by the Holy Spirit and marked as Christ's own forever." And, again, "Amen."

And so it was, with water dripping from my head down my neck into the cottony white collar of a borrowed baptismal gown, my life of faith began. The baptizer passed me back to the waiting arms of my parents, but I was no longer only theirs. I had been placed in a greater embrace. Promises had been made: by my parents, to raise me to seek and know God; by my congregation to remind me that belonging to God meant belonging to all of God's people; by God, to love me as God's own child, forever.

I did not choose this path for myself, but as anyone chosen out of love knows, there would be time enough for a million choices of my own.

CHAPTER TWO

I wanted to be a beginner for as brief a time as possible. The sweet taste of tango's walking-made-dancing magic was still fresh on my lips, but I knew my imagination was picking up the slack between my clumsy steps and the dancing feeling of that enchanted night at *Strictly Tango*. The new girl, the one with the stars in her eyes, might get asked to dance once or twice for the novelty of it, but eventually she'd be expected to know what she was doing.

In my eagerness, I headed out to the very first class offered in Vancouver that very week, which turned out to be a Monday evening class in a church basement in Kitsilano, just across the bridge from my West End apartment. I arrived at the venue a few steps behind another prospective student, a well-dressed young man who held the door open for me at the top of the stairs. I wondered if I could take this gentlemanly act as a sign that he'd already taken lessons.

As we wound our way through the maze of basement hallways, he introduced himself as Thor and seemed pleased that I immediately made the connection between his name and the Norse God of Thunder. We found the main hall that would serve as our studio by following the sound of the music. About a dozen students were already dancing in the centre of the hall. We paid our drop-in fees and were directed to take seats at a table on the far side of the hall. They needed, we were told, a few minutes to revise the lesson plan to accommodate "absolute beginners," and I felt like I was being sent to stand in the corner for something that wasn't my fault.

The chairs and tables were of another era. There were the banners hanging on dusty dowels here and there, burlap and felt reminders of my childhood Sunday School. "Bloom Where You Are Planted" with a bright yellow daisy, and "Trust in the Lord" with fat balloon letters that might have been cut out by a six year-old. I half expected my childhood Sunday School teachers to appear, with broad smiles and macramé-strapped guitars, getting us warmed up for a round or two of "Kumbaya".

When the instructors had concluded their impromptu meeting, Brent—who turned out to be the principle instructor—busied himself with the students already practicing on the dance floor, while William—an understudy of sorts, I assumed—came to the table where Thor and I were patiently waiting We quickly rose from our chairs, ready to begin but not sure if we were to make our way to the dance floor to join the others or not. Not, as it turned out, very definitely not.

"I would like to begin," he said, gesturing us to sit down again and pulling up a chair for himself, "with a few comments." He spoke reverently, passionately, and with capital letters. We learned about The Walk, The Breath, The Connection. He spoke of the necessity to dance with an embrace so complete that it felt to the partners as if they were breathing into a shared set of lungs, moving as one body with four legs. There was a lot of repetition, a lot of searching for the right words in his monologue. As I recount my own tale of tango, I can sympathize with the striking inadequacy of words. At the time, it was hard to be patient with the effort he was making to reveal, describe, explain, decode, emphasize, and so on. "Walking is the study of a lifetime. I've been studying it for years and still cannot say that I've mastered it. I may not live long enough to master it!"

It appeared he might not live long enough to put it into words, either. I had come to this church basement on a rainy Monday night to dance, not sit. Thor, God of Thunder, stifled a yawn and shifted in his Sunday School chair, making a creaking sound against the floor. Was my body language as obvious? I decided it would be best to give up on dancing, resign myself to a verbal lesson, and make the best of it.

The superlatives and repetition bordered on tiresome, but I started to appreciate just how important it was to William to convey his love of the dance. Someone not listening carefully might hear smugness in both his tone of voice and the content of his monologue. He seemed to be implying that only those willing to devote a lifetime to tango, like himself, should deign to set foot on the dance floor. I chose to hear humility in his voice. I chose to take him for a man who'd embraced a craving he wasn't sure he'd ever be able to satisfy.

The greater part of the first hour of the class was spent thus, with William talking and two "absolute beginners" seated, obediently listening. I had so thoroughly given up the idea of dancing that it came as a surprise when he stopped, stood up, and announced, "It's time to dance." He gestured for another assistant to join us, a tall, thin woman who'd been helping with the more advanced dancers. The four of us made our way to a narrow alleyway of space between the table and chairs and the back wall of the basement. It seemed an impossibly small space to dance in. As it happened, the space requirements for the "dancing" portion of the lesson were even smaller than this thin margin on the edge of the hall.

The second assistant, Jane, took Thor to the other end of the narrow space we'd claimed for this part of the lesson. I stood with William, who smiled, formed his arms into a welcoming embrace, and nodded. I stepped toward him, placed my left arm over his shoulder and my right hand in his. Connection, I thought. Breath, I thought. Unity, I thought. All I could do was think. William had painted so vivid a picture of the tango ideal that I felt utterly paralyzed. Under the shadow of expectation, I had become incapable of taking a deep breath.

Our embrace was the very definition of awkward. The more he said, "Relax," the more my skin prickled with discomfort. "Relax... Just breathe... Relax... Relax." My shoulders tensed. I felt my stomach tighten, then my throat. When his words failed to have the desired effect, he tried another approach. "Forget about the arms," he said as he released my hand and shrugged my arm gently from his shoulders. "Think only of the breath." This was worse by far, and even more awkward. I became acutely aware of the movement of the fabric of his shirt against the fabric of my dress. We were almost motionless, yet I felt friction in that narrow textured space. The only action was the rise and fall of our chests against each other. Rise and fall, rise and fall. Breathing. Just breathing. But not together. The effect was more r-rise and f-f-fall, r-r-rise and f-fall.

We stood in that narrow, awkward space for a small forever. We were chest to chest, but inside I was cringing away from the place where my body touched his. Instead of unified breath and silken unity, we took stuttering breaths, with all the ease of cold, bare skin rubbing against a wet, woolen blanket.

Whether he'd had enough of me or got a signal from Brent or Jane that a switch of partners was in order, William abandoned our awkward communion for a turn with Thor. I found myself, quite suddenly, face to face with Jane, whose smile was the broadest part of her anatomy. I felt thick and clumsy as I struggled to arrange myself within and around her delicate frame. If it was hard to find a common breath in contact with William's broad chest, I feared it would be impossible next to Jane's rib cage. To her credit, we managed to move in a walking step for a few minutes, back and forth in that narrow alley of space. We did not share the same lungs. We did not move as a single body with four legs. But we walked. I did not fall headlong into the humiliation that felt so close at hand and for that I was grateful. But the night was not over.

As the clock on the back wall neared nine o'clock, Brent drew the class—including Thor and me—into one big circle for a final short lecture and demonstration. His style was as far from William's as possible. Where William had spoken quietly and eloquently in obvious reverence for the dance, Brent strutted and gestured and blustered his way through something of a dramatic monologue. I remember his posture and volume, but not his words. His words were struck from my memory by what happened next: He asked for a volunteer from the class, a volunteer for a demonstration. He picked me.

The music began and I was thrust into motion, without a moment's attention to the quality of our embrace or the unity of our breath. He addressed the class loudly as we danced. "All you need to do is..." and I found myself spinning around him. "For the *boleo*, you only have to..." and my leg flipped and flopped behind me. I surrendered to his force out of necessity, instinctively knowing that I risked injury if I didn't make myself as malleable as possible. I was a crash-test dummy, heading straight for a brick wall at breakneck speed in a car controlled by a dedicated maniac.

Mercifully, the music stopped. Students clapped. Brent beamed and thanked me for my willingness to participate in the demonstration. I turned my face to the floor, not wanting my unease to show, and found my way back into the circle.

For all appearances I had danced well. Brent was still beaming. The class had clapped. But I felt sick to my stomach. I had come in search of tango magic, and found something else entirely. My mind swam as I tried to settle my thoughts. I thought of the time I saw my reflection in the distorted mirrors of a funhouse, twisted and grotesque, me and not me. This was and was not tango. There was truth here, and earnestness, and dedication, and something so far from the magic I craved that it left a bitter taste in my mouth.

Another church. Another time. In an alcove at the very front of the sanctuary, there is an enormous tank of water. There are steps leading into the tank, and room for two adults to stand beside each other in the water. The tank has been filled with water, waist-deep, neither warm nor cold, and smelling of chlorine. Once upon a time, a well-meaning artist painted a mural around the alcove—a lakeside scene from the church's youth camp in the Muskokas. I've been there and recognize the spot, but it feels a million miles away.

I'm standing at the top of the steps, waiting for my pastor to call me into the water. I wish they'd warned me about the robe I would have to wear. It is thick and itchy, made of dense polyester, thick enough to ensure no body parts are be discernible once it's wet. There are lead fishing weights sown into the hem to make sure it doesn't bubble up irreverently when I step into the water. The texture makes my skin crawl. I feel like I'm wearing someone else's bathing suit.

A moment ago, I stood in front of the congregation and spoke careful words that I'm trying hard to believe. I chose my words carefully because I do not want to insult my father who is sitting in the back pew of a church very much not his own. Real or imagined, I sense his discomfort. I affirmed my parents' love and prayers and the mark of my first baptism. I try to trust that they understand why I'm doing this now, why I've chosen a baptism of my own.

The pastor gestures for me to walk down the steps into the tank. I try to ignore the sensation of wet polyester clinging to my skin as I cross my arms over my chest and let myself fall back into the water. I try not to be too heavy as my pastor pulls me up again. There is water in my eyes and ears and the world is muffled. I climb the steps out of the pool, weighed down by sodden polyester and disappointment. I feel my own discomfort now, and wonder why this feels so inadequate. I had been so sure.

CHAPTER THREE

Falling back on the happy memory of the *Strictly Tango* milonga, and with a new willingness to wait more patiently to start lessons, I registered for the next beginner series at the *Strictly Tango* studio and started counting down the days to the first class.

On the Sunday of the first lesson, I walked the three kilometers from my apartment to the studio and arrived fully twenty minutes before the class was due to begin. The moment I stepped through the doors, it was clear that this was no milonga. The room was stark and a little frayed around the edges. The once-upon-a-time sumptuous velvet sofa revealed itself now as faded and threadbare, sagging, and not a little bit sad. The bar was littered with empty wine bottles and an overturned coffee mug. The windowsill eyes of the studio looked in with grey indifference where once they glimmered with dark delight. I thought of the first time I returned to my childhood home as an adult; how everything had felt smaller, diminished, hollow.

The room brightened noticeably when Talia arrived—a strikingly beautiful Iranian woman, *Strictly Tango*'s founder and lead instructor. She stretched her arms toward me, gently embraced me by the shoulders and kissed my cheeks, right then left. "Ah, Sandra! Welcome!" I was surprised she'd remembered my name. She excused herself to begin her preparations, stopping first at the stereo to fill the room with music. I set my bags on the floor and dropped into the sofa, uncertain as to what to do next. Talia began to pull an enormous dust mop back and forth across the dance floor, sending swirling pinpricks of light into the air. I took off my coat, unwrapped the scarf from around my neck, took a deep breath, and fiddled with the ribbon laces of my shoes.

Gradually, other students arrived, coming into the room tentatively or with feigned confidence. Every one moved about very individually, which was particularly strange to observe in the couples that had arrived together. There were brief introductions, and a strangely intense focus on the intricacies of exchanging street shoes for dance shoes. We all knew exactly one thing about each other: We were here to learn tango. This implied, quite naturally, that we would soon be holding each other in ways generally considered inappropriate between strangers.

These solitary observations were interrupted by the sudden silence of the stereo. With a large arm gesture and few words, Talia gathered us around. We shuffled into a wobbly ring of attention around her while she calculated if there was an even number of males and females in attendance, her finger tapping out a staccato rhythm in the air, *one-two, one-two, one-two.* She was obviously excluding from the count the not-particularly-tall but very definitely dark-and-handsome man standing at the fringe of the group. I recognized him immediately as Hernando, the mutual friend who'd set up my "first date" with tango and Talia's teaching partner. He'd arrived without my noticing. We smiled and nodded at each other across the room, so as not to interrupt Talia who was now describing how the class would proceed.

It was good to see him again, just across the studio from me after a distance of several years. In much the same way the sight of an old family photograph can conjure up a rapid rush of memories, so the history of my acquaintance with Hernando flashed through my mind. We'd met through my boyfriend at the time, a long ago summer afternoon at Lighthouse Park. Hernando made a strong impression, with his Latino good looks and with the stories he could tell. He had ended up in Vancouver after a monumental cycling trip from his homeland, Argentina, to Alaska. Having biked along the western coasts of South, Central, and North America—a journey that included close encounters with Central American guerilla soldiers— he clearly had a powerful passion for adventure.

He was handsome and compelling, but his way in the world scared me. He'd cajoled my boyfriend into jumping off the cliffs with him that day. To clear the rocks below and land safely in the water, they had to take a running leap over the edge. Hernando let out a long yell as he threw himself head-long over the cliff. His voice did not carry a hint of shock or fear; it was a yell of unfettered delight. I remember the yell well because I could not bring myself to watch him jump.

Here he was, some ten years later, teaching Argentine tango. Talia introduced him to the group, gestured for him to step forward, then disappeared briefly to begin the music again. A slow, luxuriant music filled the room. "We will begin," she said, "With a demonstration." They approached each other slowly, moved gently into each other's arms, and stood together in a mutual embrace. There was a long pause before the first step. They stood together, in a relaxed stance, breathing together, waiting, and listening. The class watched in complete silence.

To watch an experienced couple dance tango alone, with the whole of the dance floor to themselves, is to stand still in time. The music and motion of the dance cast a spell, suspending awareness of anything mundane. I felt myself gradually reduced to the simple sum of eyes and ears and soul. Unlike my milonga experience, where my eyes revelled in the cascading movements of a dance floor full of dancers, here I could maintain a singular focus on the two-as-one pair before me. I felt strangely weightless and deeply aware. Though I was most definitely standing perfectly still on the sidelines, some kind of magic allowed me to participate in the dance unfolding before me.

They moved in intricate patterns, turning where the music turned, crafting lines and curves on the dance floor with their feet, sometimes stepping with the rhythm and sometimes offering a physical counterpoint to the beat. With the dance floor entirely to themselves, there was no need to look out for the movements of other dancers. They took full advantage of this liberty, taking long lunging steps and wide curving turns that would be impossible on a crowded dance floor. Their movement together was seamless.

They danced with eyes closed, or so it seemed. They seemed to be relying on some fine-tuned visceral awareness of the dance floor, as if physical vision would interfere with how they felt their way through the music. Their faces bore expressions of complete focus, shifting ever so slightly now and then, with a furrowed brow or the hint of a smile, shimmering briefly on the surface of a deeper calm. Around this focal point of intensity, their bodies curved and spun, turned and flowed, quickly and slowly, gently and forcefully. The intimacy was palpable.

I focused my attention on Hernando for a moment, struck by the quality of his focus and the way he moved. His dark Latin looks lent a particular authenticity to the dance, but there was a deeper authenticity at work. Dancing, here on the worn floorboards of the *Strictly Tango* studio, his movements were infused with a passion and intensity completely congruent with the character of the man I had met that long ago day in Lighthouse Park. The passion that inspired a million-mile trip from Argentina to Alaska, the zest for adventure that propelled him over the cliffs at Lighthouse Park, were contained somehow in the strength and grace of his dancing. His steps were strong and intentional, but appeared to be entirely uncalculated. He was not leaping over a cliff edge with reckless abandon, but he seemed to be moving with an instinct that might well come from the same place. He was not telling tales of mountains and jungles and coastal rainforest, but he was giving expression to an interior landscape as fraught with danger and as beautiful as any he'd encountered on his grand adventures. Hernando poured himself into this dance, into this moment of tango, and tango made room for him. This time, I could watch. Barely.

The music stopped too soon. We took a collective breath. As I became aware again of my surroundings, I gazed around the studio and took in the wide range of expressions on the faces of my classmates. Expressions ranged from the beaming smiles of the truly inspired to the furrowed brows and skeptical grimaces of the deeply intimidated.

"Let's begin," said Talia.

For a solid hour, I struggled in the crazy-making space between deeply inspired and deeply intimidated. I listened to every instruction, every correction, as if my life depended on it. Whereas Hernando's tango was infused with passion, mine was infused with clamouring insecurity and desperation. He had complete focus. I had all the focus of a dashboard bobble-head figurine. Cravings for perfection danced with convictions of clumsiness, twisting and tripping over each other in my brain. I would feel a surge of hope at a well executed left-right-left-right. Mere steps later, I would collide with my partner in a collapsed embrace and suffer an overwhelming surge of discouragement. Elegance was being trampled by insecurity and it did not make for a pretty dance.

I longed to dance beautifully. My feet ached from the effort. My brain ached from the effort. For my feet to find their way across the floor, my brain had to forge new connections. I had been walking since I was nine months old, but crafting beauty out of simple steps was completely foreign to me. Like a crayon-wielding three-year old willing herself to colour inside the lines, I bit my lip in concentration and had to remind myself to breathe. Sweat gathered in the small of my back, the muscles of the back of my legs felt stretched and strained, I felt crippling cramps in the arches of my feet. My shoes traced jagged, stuttering lines on the floor and I struggled not to give in to feelings of hopelessness.

Class ended. My ragged dream and I had made it through our first tango lesson. "Very good, everyone," said Talia. "The next class starts in twenty minutes. You are welcome to stay until then and practice what you've learned." Some of those attending the next lesson had already stepped onto the dance floor to warm up. They were also in early stages of learning the dance, but looked accomplished compared to our lot. With no desire to spend another minute on the dance floor with my uncooperative body parts, I retreated to the sofa in the corner of the studio to take my shoes off and gather my thoughts.

"Sandra! Let's dance!" Hernando stepped in front of me, blocking my retreat to the velvet comfort of the sofa.

A dozen thoughts tried to form words on my lips. The competing signals rendered me idiotically mute. *Me? You want to dance with me? I couldn't possibly. I'm a klutz. I can't dance. Did you not just witness a full hour of my horrific inadequacy on the dance floor?* And yet, from some other corner of my soul, came the urge to say, *Yes! Yes! Yes!*

"Let's dance," he said again, his deep brown eyes looking entreatingly at me from under raised eyebrows.

I managed a nerve-studded reply, "You want to see if I've learned anything today?" I tried to throw in light-hearted laugh, but failed.

"Class is over. This is for fun," he said as he raised his arms in the invitation of embrace.

I accepted, and stepped into his embrace. I placed my left arm across his shoulders, resting my hand on his right shoulder. My right hand tentatively reached up to take his left to complete our frame. I trembled from the effort to do everything just right, and from the fear that I was about to humiliate myself completely.

At precisely this moment, Hernando stepped back and broke the embrace, gently shaking his head from side to side, smiling. "Why so nervous?" Clearly, the embrace felt as awful for him as it did for me. I had given it my best effort, and failed. He urged me on, with his captivating Argentine accent, dark eyes, and warm smile. "Sandra, you are trying too hard. Class is over. This is for fun. We are friends. Now, we dance as friends, not as instructor and student." Again, he offered his embrace.

I stepped toward him again. He whispered, "Relax." He pressed and released and pressed and released his grip of my right hand, helping me find the right strength of connection for our embrace. And again, he whispered, "Relax." He took a deep breath. I took a deep breath. *Inhale. Exhale. Inhale. Exhale.* His breath warmed the small space between us. When we were breathing in sync with each other, he stepped. Without thinking, I stepped into the space he created. Again, and again, I stepped into his lead. His confidence, so unlike the hesitant lead of my fellow beginners, inspired trust. With each step I released a little more tension; muscles relaxed, shoulders began to unclench. I became more and more aware of my breath and found its rhythm. My inner monologue of discouragement was silenced, leaving space within me for trusting, and movement, and music. I was no longer trying to colour inside the lines. I wasn't trying to colour at all. I was colour.

We danced for four, maybe five minutes. When the music stopped, we took a few more minutes to catch up on the years, to get reacquainted. While we were talking, while my mouth was relaying an abbreviated chronology of the events of the past several years, my heart was humming a little song of thanks: *We danced! We danced! I* can *learn to tango. I* will *learn to tango.*

Two pairs of students were standing nearby, obviously hoping for some of Hernando's time and advice. Our brief conversation ended with a quick hug and I readied myself to leave. After I had packed up my belongings, I lingered in the studio just long enough to see the next class begin. The Level Two dancers were circled around Talia and Hernando, eagerly awaiting the demonstration that would begin their own lesson. The studio was still void of fairy tale splendour, the sofa was still faded and worn, and the window eyes of the city, now darkened by autumn's early nightfall, still lacked the sparkling interest I had imagined in them the night of that first milonga. But the spirit of the room was charged. A silent chorus of expectation rose from those gathered as Talia and Hernando began to dance. Eyes were riveted.

It was hard to leave. My appetite for tango had been thoroughly whetted and I had not had my fill. I was perhaps only slightly closer to achieving a flawless first step, and without a doubt that there were a great many hours of stumbling and tripping ahead of me. I knew my inner battle against fear and insecurity was far from over. But, as I walked home in the pouring rain, I was truly, deeply, and desperately sure that I would learn to dance. I had tasted something mysterious and powerful, and I wanted more.

To hear the story told, God has loved me since before I was born. My favourite version of the story is in the Psalms, the one where God knit me together in my mother's womb. I like the idea of a God who knits. Loving God was as natural as loving my parents, or ice cream for that matter. I was in love long before I knew that what I felt about God—or my parents, or ice cream—was something called "love." As in all relationships, sometimes things get complicated. This usually happens so gradually that by the time you've realized something has changed, it doesn't look anything like love anymore.

My mother tells the story of a summer day when I—all of three or four years old—had been particularly naughty. I don't recall all the details of her story—for instance, I couldn't tell you what my particular transgression was that day—but the story's punch line is as vivid to me as any memory of my own. "After dinner, you had the nerve to ask if we could go to Dairy Queen for dessert! Dairy Queen! After being so bad earlier in the day; as if nothing had happened!" I picture myself—all red-hair and freckles, with a bit of sunburn on my nose—sitting on my booster seat at the kitchen table, having eaten my vegetables and cleared my plate like a good girl, trying to make sense of my mother's reaction.

It's impossible to say at what point my under-standing of God started getting messed up, but if I had to put a tack on the timeline of my life to mark the occasion, this is where I would put it. Up to that point, I understood that when I said "I'm sorry" and meant it with all my heart—because I really, really, really didn't want to disappoint anyone, least of all my mother—I was forgiven, I-love-you forgiven, ice-cream-for-dessert forgiven. This new evidence—my mom's reaction to what seemed to me a perfectly reasonable question—set the little cogwheels of my three- or four-year old brain to work. How could I reconcile unconditional love with the hopelessness I felt at that moment? If it wasn't enough to be sorry, what was enough?

CHAPTER FOUR

I came to tango in the fall. Like every autumn in Vancouver, it was grey and rainy most of the time, which doesn't bother me at all, though most people don't believe me when I tell them that. Once upon a time, when I was a child asking for lullabies, my mother taught me to listen for rain against the windows at night, which might account for some of my love of the rainiest season. But the principal reason I love autumn is because it was at that time of year that I started to live again.

In my mid-twenties, I fell headlong into a chronic, deep, and debilitating depression. I had been stumbling around the edges of depression all my life—something I realized in hindsight, of course—but at this particular juncture in time I had unwittingly set myself up for a fall greater than any I had weathered up to that point in my life. It came near the end of what I had been calling my sabbatical. I had put my carefully-planned career on hold for a year to study theology at a graduate school on the west coast. I set out for Vancouver from Toronto with my little Plymouth Horizon packed tight with my father's old theology textbooks, my mother's old guitar, a computer, and ski equipment—ready to put five thousand kilometers between me and what I called home. I was set to savour a yearlong retreat of sorts, a time-out to fortify my faith, confirm my career path, learn how to play guitar, and ski as much as possible.

A lot happened that year. In the first semester, I remembered how to play as well as how to study. I had been absent from both worlds for some time; it felt good to be back. Billy Graham's nephew taught me how to play touch football, sketching out plays on his chest as if I could interpret the path of his finger and move across the field accordingly. I was hopeless at it but it didn't matter; they let me play anyway. I studied at the beach whenever I could. I learned how to play the guitar. I daydreamed, made new friends, helped with the weekly student newspaper, and spent time at all three local mountains once the snows came. In my theology classes, I was learning a new vocabulary—not just for academic study, but for personal reflection and critical thinking about my faith. I gave myself permission to ask big questions. I didn't know how dangerous that could be.

Something shifted with the turn of the calendar year. I started thinking about what would come after this yearlong sabbatical. I wanted more time to think and feel and ask big questions. It occurred to me that I could delay my return to a now uncertain career path, stay in Vancouver, maybe do the whole Master's program. Suddenly there was more at stake. Instead of learning for the sheer pleasure of it, I launched myself into class work with all the fervour of an achievement-oriented perfectionist, aiming for top grades and taking on an extra heavy course load. I signed up for summer school

Hebrew to take care of the biblical languages requirement of the degree as efficiently as possible—two full terms of Biblical Hebrew in eight weeks. Students called it "suicide Hebrew," which I thought was a tasteless exaggeration.

In spite of the frenzied effort I was pouring into my studies—or because of it—the big questions I was asking of life got bigger. Monstrous, in fact. And more insistent. When I could no longer articulate the questions, when all the permutations of *why*, and *how*, and *who am I*, and *who am I to God*, and *who is God, anyway* were unable to contain my angst, my life fell apart. I couldn't attend class. I couldn't study. I couldn't sleep. I couldn't get out of bed. I lost my appetite. I lost my place in the world. I didn't care, and I cared so much I couldn't bear it.

The carefully constructed notions of my faith, lined up like neatly-labeled boxes stacked in tidy towers, came crashing down around me. Understanding had abandoned me. Words had lost their meaning. Life had lost its meaning. Yet there remained a delicate sliver of faith, about the size of three little letters—G-O-D—written in a three-point font in the lowest corner of an otherwise blank billboard. God had become very, very small.

I lived in this depression for years. I sought help, and help sought me, without any lasting success. Most of these years are a blur, assorted indistinct memories fading in and out of grey. I couldn't tell you anything about the weather, about how I wore my hair, about significant events. I have entries in my address book from this time, names and addresses of people whose faces I cannot recall. Doctors signed papers saying I would never work again. I remember this: I cried every day; I was given fifteen different medications over five years with no positive outcome; every day of those years my mouth tasted either of metal or cotton or bile; I couldn't bring myself to buy Q-tips because it overwhelmed me to think of living as long as it would take to use the whole box. And one more thing: When I hit bottom, I got the help I needed to start over.

Help took the form of an agnostic non-practising Jewish psychologist who didn't care about meds or childhood history or religious baggage, but cared very much about what I thought about myself and about the world I lived in. Since these thoughts had brought me to the point of an emergency hospital admission for self-inflicted wounds and suicidal visions, he had a pretty good case for questioning my judgment. Of course, it took him a while to convince *me* of this. Depression has a way of ensuring that the bleakest, blackest perspective on life looks like the truth.

We met on the Monday after I had been admitted. By this time, I had told my grey and hopeless tale a dozen times or more to various medical professionals—what meds I was on, who my psychiatrist was, how I ended up in hospital. He cut me off. "I don't need to know any of that," he said. "What are you feeling right now? What are you thinking right now?"

I could not answer him. He started talking, probing, asking simpler questions, asking more detailed questions, and somewhere in the middle of him talking and me struggling to think, I heard this through the noise: "It doesn't have to be like this."

It doesn't have to be like this. I was sitting in his office, twenty feet or so from the hospital room I occupied, though to say I "occupied" the space was an exaggeration—I was as absent as it is possible to be while still alive. I had no belongings of my own. I was allowed only a toothbrush, toothpaste, and a comb. I was wearing doubled up hospital gowns labeled "Property of Vancouver General Hospital" and hospital-issue knee socks—machine-knitted tubes with no definition for the heel or toes. My wrists were bandaged, covering wounds that I had scratched into my body with my fingernails in an effort to feel something, anything, other than the excruciating numbness of depression. *It doesn't have to be like this.*

He was calm, confident, relaxed, and spoke with a deep baritone voice. He waited.

"I want to believe that," I said, eventually. I hardly recognized my voice.

"That's where we'll start then," he said.

Our journey together lasted a few years. Daily meetings in the hospital were replaced with out-patient appointments, first twice a week, then once a week, every other week, and so on, until we were meeting once a month. He was as ruthless as I was resistant. He cut through my depressive thoughts, pulling them apart, forcing me to answer, over and over and over again: *Is that true? Where's your evidence for that? How can you back up that thought?* He taught me to recognize when my thoughts needed to be challenged, gave me tools to separate lies from truth, and forced me to practise, practise, practise, until I came to see the power of the expression, "the truth will set you free." "Seek Truth" became my motto, not only in times of crisis but every day, all day. It is the hardest work I've ever done. It is still hard.

It was autumn when I started noticing the weather again. I imagine that God nudged me into this time of awakening in Vancouver's starkest months to gently ease me into life beyond the dim world of depression. I needed autumn's quiet beauty to learn how to see and feel the world again—the slick yellow of autumn leaves against rain-blackened tree trunks, the way the slimmest light creates a thousand shades of grey on the water, the feel of misting rain upon my skin. Nearly twenty years have passed since that first fall and every autumn I remember how it felt to find myself alive again.

The black dogs of depression still clamour at my door, but I've learned how to watch for the signs of their approach and know what to do to keep them at bay. Most of the time. There are times when they break through the door and drag my fragile soul toward the pit I swore I would never fall into again. This is what happened in the summer before tango.

In June, friends who had become family to me moved across the continent to pursue a new career opportunity, taking with them their two daughters—girls whom I had known from their first breaths to their first steps, girls I loved with all my heart. It was beyond me to be excited for their new adventure when my heart was breaking from the loss.

Also in June, I received an email from a cousin who'd been estranged from the family for over twenty years. She explained this decades long withdrawal by sharing her story of sexual abuse at the hands of her father and elder brother, my uncle and cousin. Into that broken silence, others revealed secreted stories of sexual abuse within the broader family. Everything I had believed about my father's family—a good family, a faithful family—was thrust into the confusion of grief.

At the end of the same month, a routine mammogram revealed a "suspicious mass." As I waited for the results of a follow-up ultrasound, my mind swam with the implications of a cancer diagnosis: *How does a self-employed, single woman who lives five thousand kilometers from her family get through cancer treatments?* I left a voicemail message for my brother and his family: "Don't panic... It's likely nothing... But I thought you should know I might have breast cancer." He did not call back. I should have told him that a little panic would have been nice. My parents offered support, inviting me to live with them and have cancer treatments in Toronto, a commutable distance from their new condo. I was sick at the prospect of leaving Vancouver—my home of nearly twenty years. When it was confirmed that the initial finding was a false positive, I was relieved but could not shake the sense that I was more alone than I thought I had realized.

I could practically smell the black dogs at the door. I threw everything at the wretched beasts: *Eat right, Sandra. Exercise. Get more sleep. Journal. Seek truth. Seek truth. Seek truth.* Then I got pneumonia, lost my appetite, had no energy for exercise. All I could do was sleep and journal, and the truest truth I could come up with as I scrawled across the blank pages in front of me was that the world was a very, very broken place, and I was worn out by all the brokenness. I had not been this close to the edge of the pit in years and I was terrified. Like a drowning woman grasping for something, anything, to keep her afloat, I grasped for some new means of coping with the grief, some new way to battle the darkness. The two new things placed within my reach were quilting and tango, the chalk and cheese of recreational therapies.

A friend and former colleague invited me to join her for a quilting class at the Thread Bear Quilting Shop. "We never see each other any more and this way we'll get to see each other every week *and* do something creative." So it was that I spent most of the summer battling the chaos of grief with tiny patches of fabric cut into perfect squares, laid out in orderly patterns, and sewn along careful, straight lines. Some of grief's dust settled in the reassuringly precise ninety-degree angles of those carefully stitched squares. I took comfort in the patterns that I laid out on the dining table, squinting to see the balance of light and dark in the design. Playing with colours, textures, and patterns focused my thoughts on beauty. Quilting gave me a still point to hold onto until my grief subsided like the hysterical toddler who finally cries herself to sleep after an all-consuming tantrum.

Another friend took me kite flying on a windy August afternoon and, somewhere between running after the kite I kept dive-bombing into the tidal flats, and treating me to supper, told me he was thinking of learning how to tango. Under the influence of more fresh air than I had tasted in weeks, the feel of wind and water against my skin, and the unexpected return of my appetite, I thought it was the most glorious idea. I asked my ex-boyfriend for Hernando's number, called him, and scribbled the details of the next dance on a slip of paper pulled out from under a pile of fabric scraps. *Strictly Tango, 505 Hamilton Street, nine o'clock. Don't expect to dance.*

By the time the fall rains fell on Vancouver again, I had packed up my sewing machine, folded up my unfinished quilts, and tucked my fabric supply into boxes for storage. These things would all come out again, when the time was right for quilting. For now, the time was right for tango.

In the season of my greatest grief, I did not go to church. When the world first closed in on me, I tried to push on with routines that had once nourished and comforted me. I dragged myself to church on Sunday morning whether I had slept that night or not, desperate to be with people who knew God, hoping to be reminded of something that made sense, hoping for a hand to reach into my darkness and pull out whatever was left of me. Instead, they sang their happy songs and prayed their happy prayers and gave thanks for life and love and hope. I could not sing; I could not pray; I could not pretend that everything was okay. Sunday after Sunday, I wept in the back pew and felt my hope erode. To save my last scrap of hope, I stopped going to church altogether.

A friend came to me in this dark season. She did not sing happy songs or pray happy prayers or assault my senses with brightness I could not bear. She brought me to a sacred place and told me I could stay for as long as I needed. It was unlike any other church I'd known: dark, quiet, still. I wonder now if it was truly dark, quiet, and still or if I saw it this way because that's what I so desperately needed it to be.

In this dark place, someone pressed bread into my reaching hands, and said, "The body of Christ, broken for you."

In this dark place, someone touched a cup of wine to my lips, and said, "The blood of Christ, poured out for you."

In this dark place, I found myself in the presence of the bodied God, the God of flesh and blood, the God who knew what it felt like to be broken and poured out. This God understood my tears and did not leave me alone to weep.

CHAPTER FIVE

Opportunities to dress up in costumes diminish considerably after about age nine. As I flicked through the contents of my closet on the eve of *Strictly Tango*'s Hallowe'en Milonga, this decades old reality was vividly confirmed. Inspiration struck, however, when my fingers travelled far enough along the clothes bar to reveal a hot pink dress I had bought at a warehouse sale a couple of years earlier. It fit so perfectly, I couldn't resist buying it, even though it was a shade of pink far-and-away brighter than anything I had ever worn. Tonight, it was just the right shade of pink. I got to work.

First, the hair. This was not the night for a sleek Grace Kelly-esque French roll. This was a night for BIG hair. Curled and teased to its full capacity, my hair can get big enough to merit alerting the Vancouver Airport Authority to change flight patterns around the city. I went for that kind of big, but chose not to notify the authorities. Next, the accessories. I pillaged my stash of costume jewelry for the flashiest necklaces, earrings and brooches, and applied the rhinestone-studded false eyelashes that a friend had given to me as a joke. I slipped on the hot pink dress, and *voilà!* Rhinestone Barbie was ready to tango.

With my coat on, purse and shoe bag over my shoulder, umbrella clutched under my elbow, keys in one hand and the doorknob in the other, my brain did a rapid fast-forward. I saw myself at the milonga, in all the shimmering splendour of my bright pink dress, and felt suddenly sick to my stomach. I couldn't do it. Barbie was used to being the centre of attention. I was not. Carefully preserving the altitude of my hair and leaving every rhinestone in place, I stripped off the dress and put Barbie back in the closet. I slipped into the familiar comfort of a little black dress and headed for the door. Rhinestone Sandra would have to do tonight.

I made it to the venue on auto-pilot, psyching myself up for what lay ahead. If I hadn't been sure that the black dogs of depression would be trick-or-treating at my door that night, I might have stayed at home. Desperate times call for desperate measures, so instead, here I was, pressing my coat into the already crowded rack, stabbing my umbrella into the umbrella stand, and praying for some Narnia magic as I stepped from the vestibule to the dance floor.

It was more than magical tonight. The fabulous creatures of Narnia would have had some serious competition from this crowd. Everyone wore a costume. There were several pirates, various manifestations of vixens and politicians, a sailor, a flight attendant, Raggedy Ann and Andy, and a couple of Marilyn Monroes. My heart went out to the *geisha* who was so devoted to her costume that she danced in platform wooden slippers all night. It was painful to watch. I was similarly sympathetic to the witch whose costume was so truly hideous, and her face so grotesquely green and warted, that she barely danced at all. My de-pinked Rhinestone Barbie costume was a lackluster effort by comparison. I was, however, afforded the pleasure of overhearing— more than once— hushed debate on the sidelines, always starting with the question, "Is that hair r*eal?*"

I danced with Hernando, whose costume I couldn't decipher. And with a man dressed as a woman, whose name I did not know. His disguise was so thorough, I didn't recognize him again for several months. He danced remarkably well in high heels and bore a striking resemblance to Queen Elizabeth—though with a slight Romanian accent, broader shoulders, and five o'clock shadow.

I sat by the fireplace a good part of the evening, contentedly so, given the spectacle. As usual, I studied the dancers, taking mental notes of the best and the worst, making good use of the time. My attention was frequently drawn to one man, a particularly beautiful dancer, commanding in his lead, confident, and graceful. His mood and manner of dance altered with each change of partner, sometimes warm and playful, sometimes cold and serious. He was clearly a popular lead, judging from how rarely he rested and from how many eyes were turned to him in hopes of a confirmed *cabeceo* between one turn on the dance floor and another. I was careful not to add my eyes to the *cabeceo* chorus, watching him only while he danced. His costume consisted of a glittery headband that bore a combination of devilish horns and a halo.

It startled me a bit when he dropped into the empty chair beside me. I'm not sure if I sensed his desire for space or was simply accommodating the breadth of his shoulders, but I shifted my chair slightly away from him. He seemed glad for it, and sank a little more deeply into his chair. We sat silently. After a short rest, he danced again, and returned to the same seat beside me. He danced again, and returned. Each time, he acknowledged me with a slight nod and a slight smile. Nothing else about him was slight.

I fought against the feeling of intimidation, and, finally, broke the silence. "Devil or angel?"

"Hmn?" He turned his face toward me.

"The horns and the halo. Devil or angel?"

"Oh. Both, I suppose." He set his gaze on my face, with clear, strong eyes, waiting for a response.

"So, naughty, but in a good way?" *Where did that come from?* I'm not given to flirting, but something about this guy brought it out in me. He smiled.

With an angel on my right shoulder on alert for further flirtation, and a devil on my left urging the same, our conversation continued. His name was Dmitri. As if the name were not clue enough, I detected a Russian accent. My observation was quickly confirmed. Born and raised in Siberia, he'd come to Canada as an adult. I try not to make assumptions, but the cold and serious manner I had seen on the dance floor from time to time did fit the Russian stereotype. But I had also observed him dance with warmth and ease and playfulness. What to make of this Siberian tanguero?

"And you. Where are you from?" he asked.

"I'm first generation Canadian," I said, "Born of Dutch immigrants."

"You don't look Dutch," he replied.

"I might not look Dutch in this," I said, gesturing grandly at my towering hair and glittering accessories, "But you should see me milk a cow." I suspect this tidbit of wit rose up from the same source as my earlier flirtation. It went over just as well. Better. There was nothing cold or serious about his laugh.

At no point in our conversation did I hint at the favour of a dance. The prospect of dancing with The Russian did not enter my mind, not even as a remote possibility. I was still very much a novice and sensible enough to show up at milongas with no expectations. Any time spent on the dance floor was a happily received grace. Such a grace was easy to accept from Richard, the prince who had extended his hand to me on the Cinderella night of my first milonga. Similarly, occasional forays onto the dance floor with Hernando could be explained by his own gracious character, and by the fact that we shared friendship and warm memories of sunny afternoons at Lighthouse Park. I expected nothing from The Russian. More than that, I had no desire to add myself to the multitudes on the sidelines, whose glances in his direction bore a striking resemblance to desperation as the night wore on. I aspired to nothing more than sharing a bit of space and a laugh or two in the corner of a crowded room. Little did I know, this small grace of my own was greatly appreciated, and thanks would come in the form of a dance.

It was late. I had just started to untie the ribbon closure of my left shoe, just begun to ready myself to leave. Dmitri stood before me with his hand extended.

"You know I'm just a beginner, right?" I answered with my neck craned, looking up from where I was leaning over my leg, still bent to the task of undoing my shoes—as if to say, *I'll just keep undoing my shoes because you can't be serious.*

He said nothing and continued to look me in the eyes. I didn't know what to make of the look. It was neither steely nor warm. It was steady, serious, and strangely commanding. My fingers trembled slightly as I drew the ribbon laces of my shoes back into a tight bow. I paused for a moment before sitting upright, and only then looked up, half hoping he'd be gone. His gaze was unchanged. As if the angel and devil had returned to their places on my shoulders, competing thoughts entered my mind. *Don't mess this up, Sandra. There's a lot at stake here. And, Relax and enjoy it, Sandra. Go for it!* Who said what, I couldn't say.

I stood and walked with him to a gap in the line of dance. Still silent, he raised his arms to form his part of the embrace. As silently, I joined him. He was muscular across the shoulders and chest, solid, strong. I felt anchored in the frame we formed, though I can't say I felt safe. There was a power, just beneath the surface, that made me feel uneasy. *Iron fist, velvet glove,* I thought. He took my right hand, released it. Took it again, released it. He said nothing, but I knew he was asking me to relax. I hadn't realized my unease had shown itself in my body language. There would be no secrets here.

Just dance, Sandra, I thought. *Just let go and dance.* I dropped my shoulders, took a deep breath, released the breath gently, and offered my hand again. We began. After a breath or two and a half dozen steps, my attention shifted from the power I felt in the muscles that flexed against my body, to the rhythms of these muscles, contracting and releasing in turn. Shoulders, chest, hips, thighs, flexing with the flow of the music, creating arcs of movement that paralleled the strains of the bandoneon and orchestra. I was bearing physical witness to a controlled strength, one that commanded curves and pivots, steps and pauses, movement and stillness. With this shift in perspective came a shift in the quality of our embrace. I surrendered to his lead. I found myself moving with a fluidity I had not yet experienced. There was a generosity at play between us; he lent me his experience and confidence, and I lent him... me.

His manner was confident, firm, and yet somehow gentle. He did not push or pull me along, never pressed his hand into my back to guide my direction as was the practice of some leads. He led and my body responded. My body performed steps I had seen but never experienced, executing them as perfectly as if I had practiced a lifetime. *Boleos* appeared out of nowhere, with no conscious effort on my part.

The chatter and general hubbub of the room gradually faded from notice. I did not so much hear the music as feel it. It came to me through the movement of his body, which, strangely and beautifully, became the movement of my body. Transported through his flesh to mine, the music inspired a seamless synchronicity of motion. I had the sensation not so much of being led, but of both of us being drawn into the music and propelled by it, moved by a single spirit.

Dmitri brought me back to my seat by the fireplace. The jarring music of a polka-like *cortina* broke into my consciousness as it is designed to do, breaking the spell of the embrace. I think I said, "Thank you," but I'm not sure the thought got as far as my lips.

"You'll do well. You have what it takes. Keep dancing." The words settled on me like a benediction.

Unformed thoughts danced in my head, gradually taking shape as I came to my senses, seated there, by the fireplace. Thoughts danced as I took off my shoes, assembled my belongings, and made my way to my car through the first cold rains of what was now November. As I waited at red lights, accelerated on green, and shifted into reverse to slip into my designated parking spot. As the elevator groaned its way to the seventh floor. As I brushed down the towering heights of my hair, peeled off false eyelashes, and washed off whatever vestiges of The Russian's cologne still clung to my skin. As I curled up under my woolen duvet. Staccato thoughts danced, and danced, and danced.

Was this what it felt like to dance like a true tanguera? I thought tanguera was a name that had to be earned. I imagined that one day I would merit the name, after I had put in enough time and effort, after I had paid my dues in classes, practicas, and on the sidelines of milongas. Now I wondered if, perhaps, it is an achievement not subject to such banal calculations. About one thing there was no question: Surrender had accomplished what effort had not. Tonight, the movement of my body matched— mysteriously, exquisitely— the image of tango I had held before me like a Holy Grail since this love-at-first-sight affair began.

Tonight, I had danced a dance of presence and absence, a dance simultaneously visceral and ethereal, a fully embodied out-of-body experience, a paradox. How was it that I could be so completely immersed in the profound physicality of the experience, and at the same time feel as weightless as a summer's breeze? And yet, what claim could I even lay on the experience? True, I was present to each breath, each step. But I danced in spite of myself, as if I had nothing to do with it. Was I just an instrument in the hands of a master?

I had tasted a mystery. I had tasted something I had longed for without knowing its name. It was exquisite, beautiful, intoxicating, and very definitely not safe.

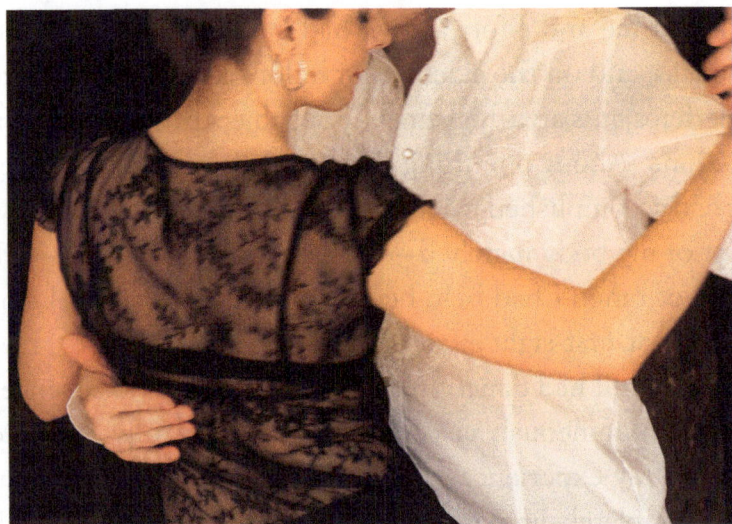

My father taught me to ask questions. My mother taught me to listen for answers. This is my inheritance. These are the tools my parents gave me, to fulfill their promise to raise their daughter to seek and know God. It is a testimony to their faith that they stand by me as I ask my own questions and listen in places they wouldn't have chosen for me.

"And what are your plans for the weekend, Sandra?" my mother asked cheerily, mid-way through what had begun as just another Saturday afternoon phone call.

"Well," I began. I had been waiting to tell them and wasn't sure this was the right moment. "I'm going to a dance tonight. I've taken up Argentine Tango and there's a social dance tonight, at the studio where I'm taking lessons."

"You're what? Let me put the speakerphone on." The phone clicks. In the background, I hear my father rustle his newspaper and clear his throat.

"Hi, Sandra!" he says. I'm glad he's home. No matter how ruffled my mother's feathers get over this, my father will bring some calm to the situation.

"I've taken up Argentine Tango, Dad. Signed up for lessons and everything."

I hear my father say, "Great!" but mom starts talking over him. "Who are you dancing with? Tan-

go? Like that stuff we saw on TV the other night, Sam? What was that show called? The one we flipped past?"

I skip the first question, knowing it will come up again, and tackle "that stuff" instead. "I don't know what you saw, Mom, but it was probably 'Dancing with the Stars' or 'So You Think You Can Dance' or some other showbiz version of tango. That's not what I'm doing. I'm learning social tango."

For a moment there's silence on the phone, punctuated by the smacking noise my mother makes when she is about to say something, changes her mind, starts again, changes her mind again, and so on—opening and closing her mouth audibly. She's choosing her words carefully, afraid of being misunderstood, unsure of the best way to begin the sermon forming in her mind. I appreciate that she's weighing her words carefully, but the longer she waits to speak, the more unnerved I am. I imagine the looks passing between my parents. Smack. Pause. Smack. Pause.

"They looked like tropical birds mating. I made your father change the channel." And there it is. Tango defined as exotic bird pornography.

"I wish you could just come with me tonight, mom," I say, though I suspect I only extend the invitation because my mother lives five thousand kilo-

meters away and is extremely unlikely to accept. "You'd see it's not like that." The conversation continues. I do my best to ease her fears, to assure her that I will be fine going there by myself. "Yes, Mom, I won't take any chances." "Yes, Mom, I'll still be going to church in the morning." Dad tells me to have a good time, though my mother will deny that when I quote him in a later conversation.

As I prepare for the night ahead, I hear, "It's like tropical birds mating," over and over in my head. I picture her coming with me to the milonga, watching for a short while and then leaving with the satisfaction of having her suspicions confirmed. "It isn't like that at all," I had said. And while it's true that social tango is a far cry from the sexually-fraught, scantily-clad tango of film and stage, I know that it is still everything my mother fears. It is vivid, exotic, sensual, intimate. How can I explain that these are the very reasons I am drawn to it? There are questions I needed to ask here. Yes, here.

CHAPTER SIX

The memory of that Hallowe'en dance with The Russian lingered the way an unsettling dream can cling to consciousness long after waking. Surface traces of the night had been washed away with soap and water, my hair had been returned to its natural altitude, and I wouldn't have recognized the scent of The Russian's cologne if a host of cosmetics clerks proffered samples of every cologne ever slathered on a tanguero's neck. Rhinestones that had sparkled by candlelight had long since been returned to the shelter of small, dark, velvet boxes, and yet, as if to compensate for the absence of any visible token, a deeply visceral memory clung to me.

To be sure, the memory held the warmth of satisfaction—the feeling of intense connection, the way the chaos of the room fell away from us, the physical presence of the music, the sense of stillness within motion. This was all part of the sweet mystery that had drawn me to tango in the first place. But there was an edge to the memory—an uneasiness that left me feeling unsettled, agitated. Seedling questions shrugged off their seed coats in the dark reaches of my consciousness, breaking up the soil, pressing to the surface, demanding light and air.

I threw myself into more classes, and attended as many practices and milongas as my schedule would bear. It's anyone's guess whether tango's increasingly prominent place in my life was fueled by unbridled enthusiasm for a new pastime, or by the unconscious need to dance faster than the questions rising within me. I was no stranger to the subtle art of denial. My newfound love of tango just happened to give my natural talent for denial a new set of tools to work with. Beautiful, sparkling, tango tools.

I devoted myself to practice. If beginner's nerves were to blame for any of this uneasiness, practice would help. If inexperience were to blame, practice would help. If I needed to become an intermediate dancer to not be treated like a rag doll on the dance floor, practice would help. I had no idea what else practice would achieve.

Around about the second month of *Strictly Tango* classes, it became increasingly apparent that the magic that transformed the left-right-left-right of walking into the art of tango was running on a rather erratic frequency in my case. I would be gliding along with all the elegance my novice steps could manage, sweetly caressing the floor with the shshsh-ing movement I remembered from that first milonga, when suddenly my foot would stick and stutter, like the visual equivalent of a sloppy, slobbery-lipped raspberry. Plb-thpl-bthpl-bth. I would trip my way into the next step or two, eventually regain my shshsh-ing poise, only to stutter again a few steps later, sometimes wrenching my knee on a pivot, adding injury to the insult of incompetence. I couldn't figure out what I was doing wrong. Like any beginner, I assumed the error was mine.

It took Talia a session or two to sort out the problem, but sort it out she did. Part way through one Sunday afternoon session, she saw my shoes stutter along the floor yet again, and the light of recognition snapped on. "Your shoes... Your shoes... I have a solution!" She rushed over to the piles of bags and boots and coats cluttering the sidelines of the studio, rummaged through her own backpack and raced back to where I stood to press a pair of bright red cotton socks into my hands. "Pull them over your toes, but not over the heels." I replied with silence and a quizzical look. "Do it. You'll see."

Daring to hope that my incompetence could be explained by a technical problem, I carefully slipped the socks over the toe-cap of my shoes. It hurt a bit to cover up the stylish stitching and ribbon embellishments of my favourite *Fluevogs*, but if vanity were the price to pay for poetry in motion, I would pay that price.

Talia stood by, offering to lead. The embrace. A pause. A breath. A step. Another. And another. My feet now glided effortlessly over the floor, with the ease of floured hands gliding over freshly rolled pie dough. In the giddiness of the sensation, I felt not like a newly minted tanguera, dancing with sensual elegance, but like a child who'd just discovered the joy of sliding across the kitchen linoleum in the new slippers Grandma knit. Talia led me forward, backward, around. Pivots no longer wrenched my knees. Instead, my body curved effortlessly around the red cottony pivot points of my newly accessorized shoes. The influence of the socks on the fluidity of the dance felt marvelous. Beyond marvelous.

If I'd had any idea what a difference it made, I would have put socks on over my shoes from the first moment I set foot on the dance floor. If I'd known socks were the solution, I would not have followed the advice of a fellow novice who told me all I needed to do was affix suede patches over the soles of any pair of heels. I'd brought my cherished *Fluevog* heels—delicious, black Lucilles with white top-stitching and silk ribbons for laces— to my local Italian shoe shop, placing them on the counter like a sacred offering. I should never have entrusted my tango future to a bit of suede and glue. With the edges of the rubber soles still exposed, any position off a perfect perpendicularity of the suede sole and the floor brought the risk of tripping, wrenching, and the unhelpful belief that I was a klutz. Now, I knew better.

The giddy sensation gave way to a growing sense of confidence. I stepped with conviction, trusting my feet to take me from one place to another gracefully. I felt light on my feet, elegant, pretty. My practice partner was no longer on edge, no longer anticipating the next clunking hiccough that would bend, if not break, the frame of the embrace and rupture our connection. Suddenly, we were able to consistently match the rhythm of the music, moving together without stuttering delays. It would have been wonderful, if he'd been able to stop laughing.

The classic image of the tanguera is one of sleek elegance. She is slim, strong, beautiful, with dark hair, dark eyes, and hot red lipstick. Her dress is black, tailored to emphasize her womanly curves, with a deep slit cutting a line from the hem to just below her hip, to accentuate the length of her legs. The long, strong, curving lines of her body are further accented by four-inch stiletto heels, sharp exclamation points ready to punctuate her every step. This is how I felt, dancing at long last with the smooth, long, gliding steps and graceful pivots I had seen but not experienced.

Now, picture this elegant tanguera wearing the bulbous, oversized shoes of a circus clown. This is how I looked.

They were just red socks, but I might as well have had glowing, fiber-optic pom-poms on my feet. My dance partner could not stop giggling. Our classmates stared and laughed. Never mind that my pivots never looked better and I was finally able to execute steps that had been impossible before, I was the object of ridicule. Me? I laughed with them. I wore the socks like a badge of honour for the rest of that class and the next, savouring the way those red cotton socks transformed every step I made.

Day by day, class by class, my dancing improved. With unstuttering steps I started to move across the dance floor with confidence and poise. It was, however, impossible to ignore the fact that I accomplished this with socks pulled over the toes of my shoes. I couldn't show up at a milonga like this—I wouldn't dare. God had blessed my cotton socks, but they had to go. It was time to go shopping.

Shoe shopping, bra shopping, and swimsuit shopping are all in the same category for me. The inevitable disappointment of discovering just how vast the gap is between dream and reality makes the whole experience daunting at best and nauseating at worst. My feet are size ten, wide, and I have larger than usual big toes. "They're good for swimming," my dad consoled me once upon a time, when I expressed my deep dismay over inheriting his foot genes instead of my mother's. The particular dimensions of my feet cause no end of trouble in shoe departments, where sizes are limited, shoes are often narrow, and what looks beautiful in size six almost invariably looks grotesque in size ten. I have great success with men's boots, which is no more helpful to me than cotton socks pulled over the toes of my rubber-soled Fluevogs.

I mustered my resolve and looked up directions to the Avalon Dance Shop, the only shoe store in town that specializes in dance shoes. Avalon, the Isle of the Blessed, Paradise. It felt like a pilgrimage. I felt like an imposter, a wannabe, she-who-dances-with-socks trying to look the part of a real tanguera. My stress levels rose the closer I got to the Main Street shop. I needn't have worried. There's an angel on the Isle of the Blessed. She has a German accent, and she knows shoes.

She greeted me as I came through the door, quickly shifting a stack of paperwork to one side on the counter and joining me on the shop floor. She was middle-aged, possibly a little past middle, modestly dressed in grey and brown, modestly coiffed with short cropped hair, looking all the more modest by virtue of being surrounded by the vibrant colour and glitter of a store packed to the rafters with ballroom, salsa, flamenco, and belly dance gear. She was quick to get down to business, and I knew right away I was in the hands of a professional.

She brought out dozens of shoes, in every imaginable colour and style, and nothing fit. I tried not to give in to despair, which is especially difficult when you're wearing disposable knee-high nylon stockings, the kind that cut off your circulation just below the knees. Despair always feels close at hand in knee-highs. After trying on and suffering through what seemed like every style in the store, Avalon felt less and less like Paradise and more and more like hell. I might have slipped entirely into the footwear equivalent of Bunyan's *Slough of Despond* were it not for the presence of that infinitely patient and divinely optimistic shop owner. She was undaunted and seemed to relish the challenge of finding shoes for what I was coming to see as grotesquely malformed feet. She met my discouragement with box after box of shoes, offered like repeated benedictions, shoe salvation. In her soft German accent, again and again, "How are they? Better?" And then, "I have something else to try, I'll be right back!"

Once or twice, the fit was good enough to merit a step or two on the small section of hardwood flooring that was set up near the back of the shop, a miniature dance floor. After a few awkward steps and the disappointing recognition of a design that pinched with the promise of blisters, the shoes would be returned to their box, wrapped again in a hush of tissue paper, and quietly returned to the shelf or storeroom. "I have another idea. Wait here." I waited.

Even the box was beautiful, black with simple elegant gold text that read like poetry. *Arika Nerguiz, Calzado Fino Artesanal, Montevideo, Uruguay.* They were made of black laminated suede, with a delicate pewter leather trim around the throat line of the toe cap. The leather was startlingly soft. I slipped my toes into the toe cap, pushed my heel into place and, after struggling briefly to find the right hole, fastened the ankle strap. One shoe, then the other. The owner and I shared a smile. She nodded toward the test floor. I stepped onto the hardwood and extended my foot in a side step. My foot caressed the floor with a gentle sweeping motion and in an instant I felt the weight of awkwardness and discomfort leave my body. The shoes so delicately and perfectly embraced the contours of my feet that I felt simultaneously weightless and completely grounded. The leather sole glided over that small patch of dance floor like silk on silk.

I was so giddy that I almost bought a tiara on my way out of the shop.

There are dark days. Heavy days. Leaden days. To-day. And every day this week. I have abandoned my morning walk along the seawall, unable to distract myself with the fresh sea air and the usually comforting walking rhythm of left-right-left-right. Tension has wrapped itself around my chest, preventing me from drawing in a full measure of air. I have learned, over the years, that there is a correspondence between my lung capacity and the grip of depression. At its worst, it is like trying to breathe with the weight of the world on my chest. This morning I bear the weight of a question for which I have no words.

I step off the seawall, down the stone steps, and across the beach to stand at the edge of the waters. The wind is cool and damp against my skin. I try again to take a deep breath. I want to pull an answer out of the air and into my lungs, to infuse my blood with light and life again, to buoy me up to where I can breathe deeply again.

"We are mere clay, but for the breath of God," says the poet.

I have dragged this fragile, crumbling, muddy version of myself to the water's edge, to stand on the wet sand and consciously inhale, and it's the breath of God I'm craving.

CHAPTER SEVEN

The exquisite fit of my first tango shoes was put to the test that weekend, at a two-day intensive workshop at the *Strictly Tango* studio. The workshop was my birthday gift to myself. It was the perfect gift: two blissful days of tango immersion, starting on my actual birthday. I felt like a child again that birthday morning, waking up full of happy anticipation, brimming with bright-eyed hope for a day that might hold special delights for me, the birthday girl. I eagerly packed a lunch, put my black suede *Arika Nerguiz* shoes in a velour-lined shoe bag, grabbed an umbrella, and headed across town in the cool damp of a wintry Vancouver morning.

December's timid morning light was just starting to filter through the studio's towering plate glass windows when I arrived. I perched on the edge of the velvet sofa to change into my new shoes. It was a risk to put on brand new shoes at the start of a six-hour dance class, but there was no question in my mind that it was worth it. The birthday girl would—nay, must—wear her new shoes. The day after I had made the momentous purchase at the Avalon shoe shop, my friends held an early birthday party for me. They presented me with a tiny pair of chocolate shoes, wrapped in bright pink foil, and an envelope of cash intended for the purchase of tango shoes.

They'd seen the sparkle that had come into my eyes since I had started to dance, and had pooled their money in a concrete gesture of loving support. My already-made purchase became their timely gift. Pulling the slender leather straps through the delicate brass buckles of the shoes was an act of thanksgiving. I felt the special delight of one who is known. How sweet it is when a gift fits so well.

Students arrived in twos and threes, casting off shells of Goretex and fleece and unceremoniously discarding waterproof boots and shoes either under the velvet sofa or higgledy-piggledy on the floor of the cloakroom. Backpacks and handbags and brownbag lunches were piled up against the walls near the couch and the bar, but the dance space itself was kept clear. Under their winter weather armour, students wore the clothes of dancers prepared for a long day of learning—simple knit skirts with layered tank-tops and t-shirts for the women, casual trousers and t-shirts for the men—practical clothes to move in comfortably all day. This wasn't the place for tango glamour. There was work to be done.

I recognized some faces from my beginner class, but there were new faces as well. We gathered in a loose circle around Talia. "Thank you all for coming, for committing to a weekend of dance," she began. "Some of you are beginners, some of you have been dancing for a while already. All of us will benefit from a concentrated time to focus on tango basics." She scanned the faces of the group as she spoke, meeting everyone eye-to-eye for a moment as if to say, *Make no mistake—I'm talking to you.* "Advanced pianists must practice playing scales... Advanced woodcarvers take the time to sharpen their tools," she continued.

It was clear that this weekend intensive would not be about fancy footwork. This was not a class in tango's shimmering adornments and embellishments. We may have been wearing dance shoes, but this was boot camp. Talia spent several minutes driving home the point. Her tone was firm, to be sure, but there was an element of excitement in it too. This was a golden opportunity for all of us. For Talia, she was excused from any need to cater to the casual student who enrolls in an evening class for a quick taste of tango; there was no need to accommodate short attention spans and consumer-driven attitudes to get to "the cool stuff" quickly. She saw this as the opportunity to help us lay a firm foundation upon which to build a lifetime of good dancing. With missionary zeal she preached a tango equivalent of the Parable of the Wise Builder—the story of the wise man who built his house upon the rock, not on the shifting sands. I was tempted to lend voice to my black-gospel soul and shout out, "Amen, sister!" but thought better of it. I just quietly nodded with the others and thanked the Divine for another perfect gift.

We began with walking exercises, stepping toward the studio mirrors, and away, forward and backward, en masse. "Eyes forward," then, "Chins up," then, "Relax your shoulders," then "Loosen your hips," Talia offered correction and encouragement from the side of the studio, watching our form and posture with experienced eyes. "The walk is the foundation of tango. Listen to the music! Step, and step, and step, and step." She clapped out the rhythm—the fingers of her left hand briskly and firmly slapping the open palm of her right hand, which she held at ear level.

As we stepped toward and away from the mirrors of the back wall of the studio, over and over again, I wondered if Talia had calluses on the palm of her left hand from a lifetime of urging students to work with the music, not against it. What discipline of patience did she practice to avoid going crazy trying to teach something that is as natural as breathing to the experienced dancer? Perhaps the satisfaction of seeing students finally grasp the notion of musicality is enough to keep going, enough to keep opening the studio for hour after hour after hour of walking, to keep clapping out the beat day after day, month after month, year after year.

I don't know how long we stayed with this exercise. There is no clock in the studio. In tango, "enough" is not defined by time. We worked at it for as long as Talia pushed us. "Walk like a cat stalking its prey, extend-*step*-extend-*step*-extend-*step*-extend-*step*," she called, clapping and stepping along with us, urging us to emphasize our steps in the same way she emphasized her speech. "Da-*da*-da-*da*-da-*da*-da-*da*," she intoned, for the benefit of those easily confused by multi-syllabic words. "And *one*, and *two*, and *three*, and *four*," for the accountants and the musically-inclined of the group. "*Feel* the music; move with the rhythm; *be* the cat."

The result our fearless leader was carefully, critically, and constantly pushing us toward was not that of a group stepping forward and backward with military precision. Far from it. Talia was trying to engender in us a way of moving to the music that transcended the mechanics of stepping on the beat. This is what The Russian had foreshadowed for me the night of the Hallowe'en milonga. When the music was light-hearted and quick, so were our steps. When surrounded by a soulful song of lament, our movements across the floor became slower, heavier, as if weighed down by a shared grief, moving at the pace of a funeral cortège. Here in class—under bright studio lights and surrounded by the unblinking critique of the studio mirrors—we worked and worked and worked to bring our clumsy brains and clumsier feet into some measure of intimacy with the rhythm, tone, and story of the music.

We might not leave the workshop that day or the next with musicality coursing through our veins, but Talia was making very sure that we would leave with an appreciation of the sheer dogged persistence it takes to get to that kind of deeply physical listening. Throughout the weekend, whenever our steps became undisciplined and chaotic, Talia would bring us back to the walking exercises, back to the music, back to the music, always back to the music.

Teaching fancy footwork would have been easier. There are instructors who do just that—using the same teaching technique with tango that they use when teaching foxtrot, waltz, or other ballroom dances. But tango cannot be rightly taught as a series of steps executed systematically to the carefully counted beat of a musical score. That's not tango. Tango is more like prayer. You can break down the act of praying into a series of steps—specific words spoken in specific postures at specific times of the day—but all you'll end up with is an outline of what prayer can look like, with no guarantee that anything meaningful is taking place. However, if prayer is understood to be a way of paying attention to the world around you in all its beauty and complexity, in the full knowledge that the Divine both listens with you and speaks to you, through every one of your senses—well, that's another sort of prayer altogether.

At some point in the morning, we moved into pairs for more walking. Pairs. Two-by-two. It was hardly a surprise to be paired up—"It takes two to tango," as the saying goes—but the result on this occasion was shocking. We'd had the luxury of spending a good part of the day with our attention devoted to coordinating only our own body parts. Doubling up every known and unknown body part in tango's embrace caused more than a little bit of trouble. For a while, the dance floor looked more like a scene from the church picnics of my youth, with three-legged races going on in one part of the studio and sack races in the other.

Things got even crazier when Talia took us from walking together in parallel to walking in cross. In parallel, the lead steps forward, *left-right-left-right*, as the follow steps backward, *right-left-right-left*. In cross, the lead and follow step forward and backward on the same feet, with the embrace shifting slightly to accommodate the parallel scissor action of the dancers' legs. In our case, there were no recognizable scissors moving across the dance floor. "Knees should pass each other closely, Rob. You're dancing like a cowboy! Get off the horse." And, "Peter, if you keep looking at the floor, you're asking for trouble." And, "Sandra, drop that shoulder and *l-e-a-v-e* it dropped."

Strangely enough, after over three hours of concentrated walking, I was surprised when Talia announced that we'd be wrapping up the morning session to take a lunch break. As I removed my shoes to follow along with some gentle yoga stretches, I sent up a prayer of thanks for the artisan shoemakers of Arika Nerguiz. My once pristine shoes were now covered in dust and had started to bulge slightly around the shape of my toes, but they were no less comfortable now than at the outset of the session. Under other circumstances, I might have been upset by how quickly my brand new shoes were showing marks of wear and tear, but any dismay was mitigated by the exquisite comfort they offered. They were, in fact, more beloved to me in this somewhat battered state. They had acquired an accomplished air that pleased me.

Students rummaged in knapsacks and panniers on the sidelines of the studio and within moments an impromptu picnic was underway in the middle of the studio. What could be easily shared was passed from one to another—carrot sticks, mandarin oranges, cookies, grapes, crackers. In spite of the simple fare, the mood was festive. No one was here who didn't want to be. We were like kids on the first day of summer camp, anticipating great things, bright-eyed and giddy. When we were about to clear away the sandwich wrappers and lunch bag debris, Talia suddenly appeared from the back room with a candle-festooned birthday cake. "Happy Birthday, to you! Happy Birthday, to you!"

I sang along, curious to learn who else shared my birthday. "Happy Birthday, dear Sandra! Happy Birthday, to you!" I was flabbergasted. These people barely knew me, and they got me cake! I don't remember the flavour or colour or shape of the cake, but I will never forget how it felt to be celebrated by strangers, to be welcomed into a community that I had not known existed mere weeks earlier.

We launched into the second three-hour block of the workshop with a warm up—walking, of course—under Talia's relentless scrutiny. There would be no backsliding into bad habits. Once she was assured that we had remembered something between our morning lesson and cake, we continued with a focus on the embrace. As always, we started with the basics.

Then Talia instructed us to walk in pairs—with one person walking and the other with both hands gently resting on the collarbones of his or her partner. "Close your eyes if you have trouble concentrating," she said, "Feel the space between you... Don't let it collapse or expand... Keep it steady." Every sense submitted itself to touch. The only space that mattered was the space between you and your partner. The intimacy I sensed between myself and The Russian on Hallowe'en was easy to understand in terms of physical proximity; the intimacy I sensed now, with a partner nearly two feet away from me and with only my palms touching his collarbone, was impossible to explain.

We finished the day with more solo walking in front of the mirrors. This time, Talia offered no critical commentary, giving us the opportunity to evaluate our reflections ourselves, leaving us with the music alone at this point in the day, letting us see for ourselves what this day of embodied listening had accomplished. We walked in and through and with the music, exhausted, but with smiles on our faces in place of the furrowed brows of the morning's first walk. The intensity, the repetition, the exercises upon exercises upon exercises were making a difference, an obvious and deeply encouraging difference.

I raced straight home after class, took a quick shower, heated up the previous night's Thai take-out for supper, and went straight to bed for a nap. I needed at least a short rest before going to the milonga that night. After six hours of dancing, I could hardly wait for more. I can still get a decent night's sleep if I head home around midnight, I reasoned. I had to be sensible about it. There was, after all, another six hours of lessons the next day.

The Sunday morning table is set with linen and silver, bread and wine. This is our church, our altar, our remembering place. We are gathered around the table, standing shoulder to shoulder in a wobbly circle, shuffling a bit, waiting. It is a vulnerable, trusting place. Here, we are no longer separated by the tidy lines of pews and aisles; here, we cannot hide behind our hymnbooks and bulletins.

In the centre of our rag-tag circle, the table is set with a timeless meal. It is a reenactment of the meal Jesus shared on the night of a betrayal that would propel him to his death. On that night, he broke the bread to serve his friends and followers, to serve the betrayer, the doubter, the one who will deny ever knowing him, and the ones who will weep bitter tears over dashed hopes. He spoke of bread and wine, of bodies and blood, of incomprehensible mysteries. We pass the silver plate around the circle, leaving our fingerprints on the silver as we feed each other. Hand to hand, mouth to mouth, we are united in our hunger, united to each other and to this man called Jesus. "Do this," he says, "In remembrance of me."

Next, we pass the silver chalice of wine around the circle, wiping it with wine-stained linen and rotating it a quarter turn before offering it to our neigh-

bour. "The blood of Christ," we say to each other, one after another. Our words and the wine are like beads being strung on a thread, a line of blood that makes us brothers and sisters of the One whose death we remember. Hand to hand, mouth to mouth, we remember our common thirst and inevitable death. The wine is cheap and strong and there is no pleasure in its sweetness. "Do this," he says again, "In remembrance of me."

This is the dance of our faith, this meal of remembrance. Here we share our hunger and thirst for a mystery beyond bread and wine. We eat and remember, taking into our very bodies the Mystery of God made human. Shoulder to shoulder, hand to hand, mouth to mouth, dancing together on the thin edge between life and death.

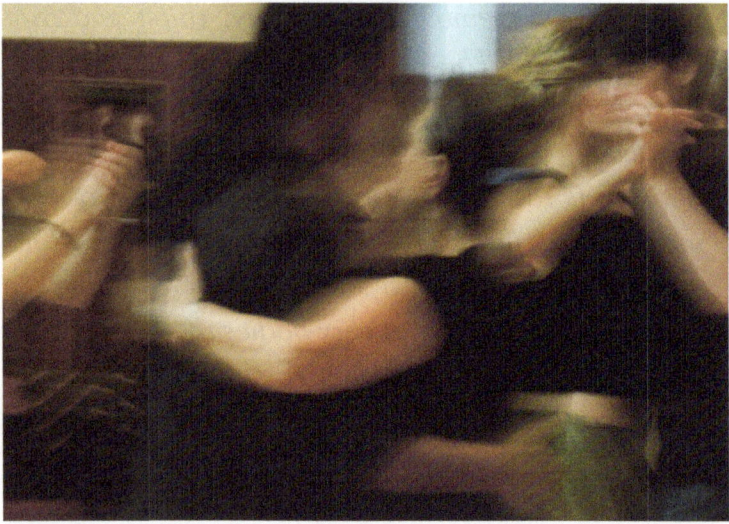

CHAPTER EIGHT

Like the stalking cat we were encouraged to emulate in our walking practice, tango started following me home after class. I indulged this new presence in my life, this playful, mesmerizing, tantalizing tango spirit. I fed it, played with it, gave it all the attention it demanded. Before long, it followed me everywhere.

Tango music gradually filled the quiet spaces of my home, steeping my formerly silent routines in a vivid, new soundtrack. In a matter of weeks, I had gathered enough tango music to fill forty hours of listening without repeating a single song. The yearning chords of the bandoneon, the heart-wrenching ballads of lost love, the playful polka-like rhythms of the milongas— tango music infused my home and seeped into my body, calling me to dance where it once sufficed to walk. *Drop your hip to allow liberty of motion to your leading leg, hold your weight on your standing leg, knees slightly bent, keep your core muscles firm, extend the foot before stepping, brush one thigh past the other, make sure your knees also pass each other closely, step just past your extended foot, allow your body to follow, transfer your weight. Step. Collect. Repeat.*

It started innocently enough. In the privacy of my little West End apartment, I practiced the stalking walk of tango, from the living room to bedroom, sometimes walking forwards, sometimes backwards. I did leg extension exercises while doing dishes, standing on one leg at a time, extending the foot of the opposite leg as if readying for a side step. *Extend. Collect. Extend. Collect. Change legs. Repeat.* Stocking feet on linoleum, preparing for greater things. In my little home—my not quite six-hundred square foot apartment with no hardwood and no mirrors—I gradually, privately, nurtured a nascent tango spirit, a tango way of being in the world. It wasn't long before this persistent, pervasive tango spirit had outgrown its six-hundred square foot play space.

The elevator in my apartment building became a private, levitating studio—seven flights of tango from the lobby to my apartment. It was no longer an irritation to live in a building with a fifty-eight year old elevator, which may have seemed speedy in its day but now had only a slight time advantage over walking up seven flights of stairs. In the elevator there was just enough room to practice extensions in all four directions. Its four walls graciously invited me to use the full space when practicing the rhythmic, *forward-side-backward-side*, grapevine-like steps of the *molinette*. Best of all, my levitating studio had the added advantage of a barre. Its simple brass rail, ringing the elevator interior, was just the right height to support the playful circular back kicks of the *boleo*.

Once the tango spirit had burst out of my little West End nest, and found its way into the impromptu elevating studio, it was only a matter of time before it forged its way into the world at large, spilling onto sidewalks, wandering into delicatessens and grocery stores.

The shopping cart took the place of the grocery basket at the Safeway, whether I was picking up four items or a cartful. This gave me a dance partner of sorts, making it ever so much easier to practice walking backwards. If another shopper or store clerk happened onto an impromptu cereal aisle practica, catching me in the act of prowling backward up the aisle like a directionally-challenged cat stalking invisible prey, I simply feigned forgetfulness, as if having just remembered an item I had recently passed by.

Standing in line at the check-out, waiting for the deli clerk, waiting for the pedestrian walk light to change, waiting wasn't anywhere near as irritating now that I could make good use of the time. The longer the wait, the longer I had to work my muscles. *Drop your hip, extend your foot, forward, backward, to the side, collect. Change sides. Repeat.* If my inner thighs burned by the time my number was called at the Santa Barbara deli counter, so much the better. I got my prosciutto, provolone, gruyère, and found myself fifteen minutes further along on the journey to stronger, leaner, dancing legs.

Before very long, I was practicing tango technique without noticing it. What had begun as a conscious effort to practice what I was learning in the studio, became something I did quite unconsciously. I had dutifully gone through the motions so often—contracting, releasing, balancing, pivoting, extending, rotating— that my muscles and joints seemed to have forgotten any other way of moving. In running shoes, rubber boots or barefoot. Down hallways, on gritty sidewalks, or along the sandy shores of English Bay. Whether stepping off the curb or out of the elevator, my steps had become infused with the form and technique of tango. It tingled through my muscles and bones, forcing the synapses of dance into every move I made.

As obvious as it was when I was caught in the act—doing *boleos* behind my shopping cart or *molinettes* in the elevator—the effects of this tango transfusion were also evident in more subtle ways. The way I carried myself had changed. My posture had become straighter, more poised. Friends asked if I'd had my hair cut or if I had done something different with my make up, having noticed a difference in my appearance but being unable to pinpoint what exactly had changed. One day, I rode the elevator with a neighbour (whose presence, regrettably, denied me seven flights of practice time) who asked if I had grown taller lately, which is quite something to ask of a woman in her forties.

The thing that had changed was the way I occupied my body. Form was replacing—or at least infusing—function. Quotidian tasks that had been, until recently, more or less subsumed into an unconscious functionality, were transformed into opportunities for beauty to express itself. Physical acts I had totally taken for granted became actions I was not only aware of, but which I deliberately chose to do artfully.

Lying in bed at night, tucked under my woolen duvet, in that twilight state of mind between active thought and the world of dreams, my muscles replayed memories of tango. Mingled with prayers of thanks for the best and most beautiful parts of the day was a visceral ache, an ache of gratitude and an ache for *more.* Perfectly still, perfectly relaxed there in my bed, my body remembered the best and most beautiful parts of the day, and remembered, too, the ache for more. I felt myself dancing to no particular music, with no particular partner—just curving and gliding, effortlessly remembering the sensation of movement in my body and feeling deliciously at ease.

Like the stalking cat we were encouraged to emulate in class, I now took my rest, curling into the warmth of my body, all but purring as I slipped into sleep.

Prayer is like water to me.

I grew up on the shores of the St. Lawrence River and I don't think I could ever feel at home without a view of the water. From my little West End nest—seven stories high and two blocks from the beach—I can watch all the moods of English Bay. The waters of the Bay can be still as glass or wild with wind, brightest blue or a million shades of grey, defiant, compliant, melancholy, riotous, hushed. My moods are often bigger than I am, and it helps to share them with the open expanses of the sea.

A vision of water came to me once, in the wee hours of a night of gut-wrenching tears. For hours I had struggled under the weight of a sadness I could not name. Sleepless and overwhelmed, I cried, and cried, and cried. All at once, lying there on a bed soaked with tears, I felt a calm come over me and with it, a vision. It was the image of me, floating in an enormous blue bowl—a hand-crafted pottery bowl glazed with the saturated blue of the Mediterranean Sea under a cloudless sky, filled with salt water as cool as the refreshment I craved and as warm as the comfort I lacked. I was naked, with my hair flowing loosely around my head, effortlessly resting in the blue. I held onto the vision as long as I could, until sleep finally claimed me.

My mother called later that day, to see how I was doing. She had been awakened in the night by an inexplicable and urgent need to pray for me. She'd slipped out of bed, eased open the glass doors to the balcony, and prayed for me by the light of the moon, listening to the rhythm of the waves splashing against the rocky shore of the river below. I told her it had been a rough night, that her prayers had been answered, that I had finally found sleep, but I did not tell her about the blue bowl.

I remember the feel of the water. My skin remembers. I remember what it felt like when my skin was the meeting place of longing and satisfaction, of giving and receiving, of sacrament, of life.

Water is like prayer to me.

CHAPTER NINE

I did not dance exclusively with shopping carts. My growing appetite for tango could not be satisfied with *molinettes* in the elevator, *boleos* at the kitchen sink, and four hours of studio classes a week. Blind love of tango propelled me to at least one milonga a week, then two, then three. I didn't go because I had to dance. I didn't even expect to dance. I went because I couldn't stay away. And because I couldn't stay away, I danced.

Tango had made its way into my wardrobe, just as it had in my daily to-and-fro. I would stroll by store windows, assessing the clothing on display. "Pretty colour. Nice design. But you couldn't dance in it." And I would walk my tango walk, right on by. Thankfully, a few items in my pre-tango closet were quite danceable. With the addition of a simple black skirt, a classic black dress, and a second less-than-classic black dress, I had enough variety to mix it up from one milonga to the next. Talia scolded me one night, for never wearing colour, but black was comfortingly unobtrusive.

The only colour accessory I employed to advantage was my hair. At that time, I had naturally wavy, nearly waist-length, strawberry-blond hair which I could manipulate into a variety of looks. An elegant French knot, straight silken locks, wild and wavy tresses, or everything pulled sleekly back into a tight bun. My changing hairstyles seemed to throw people and I often had to introduce myself to the same person multiple times.

Dressed in the little black dress du jour and my trusty brushed-suede stilettos, night by night I found a place on the folding-chair fringe that borders every dance floor. Tuesdays, it was at the Polish Community Centre. Fridays, the Dance Centre on Commercial Drive. Saturdays, it was the Maritime Museum, or Yasel's on Main Street, or *Strictly Tango* at the Hamilton Street studio, depending on whether it was the first, second or last Saturday of the month.

At every milonga, the women sat with perfect posture, poised, waiting for the subtle invitation of the *cabeceo* and the promise of an outstretched hand. Some of the men sat in the folding chairs, but most of them stood in a cluster by the bar. From there they were in the best position to survey the room for prospective partners. They awed me, these tangueros. They made me think of the Great Blue Herons I admired on my evening walks along the seawall—the way they stood there at the edge of the dance floor, elegant and aloof, quietly contemplating the night before them.

There were nights I never set foot on the dance floor. That is not to say I didn't dance. On these nights, I danced with my eyes. Sometimes I would watch a single couple for several minutes at a time as they made their way around and around the dance floor. Other times, I would shift my attention with each passing couple, enjoying a rapid-play slide show of tango vignettes. I watched for elegant footwork, good posture, and precise musicality. I took note of how distracting and awkward it looked when dancers had bad form or technique—and hoped that my own bad habits might magically disappear with the combined force of these observations and my budding vanity.

Some nights I danced only once, most often with Richard, the princely ambassador of the tango community who always had time for novices who would otherwise have spent most of the night on the sidelines. Richard was my most faithful dance partner in those early days. "Here again," he'd say cheerfully as he put on his shoes seated beside me, "Good!" It was as if he were taking attendance, measuring my commitment to the dance. Instead of a gold star by my name, I got a dance. I never had the feeling that he asked out of pity, though I dare say he asked out of charity, where charity is another word for loving-kindness. The offer of his hand seemed to be an acknowledgement of our mutual love of the dance, as if to say, "I'm glad you're here. I'm glad I'm here. Let's walk together in gladness." Yes, gladness best describes what happened when we danced.

There were nights when, quite inexplicably, I spent at least as much time on the dance floor as on the sidelines. It could have been dumb luck, an unexpected shortage of accomplished tangueras, or some conscious or unconscious acknowledgement on the part of the men that I had paid my dues in sideline time. I prefer to believe that these were the nights when I was so filled with the irrepressible tango spirit—the spirit that compelled me to show up at yet another milonga whether I would dance or not— that it overflowed, and called out to the same irrepressible spirit in the tangueros, as like calls to like.

I suppose I have to acknowledge that, sometimes, it might well have been pity that got me onto the dance floor. In which case, I'm glad for the love-is-blind infatuation with tango that afforded me the grace of rose-coloured glasses in those early days. Certainly, under tango's spell, pity looked nothing like it did in high school. It had nothing of the sad savour of swaying back and forth to the interminable Stairway to Heaven with Simon Baum in Grade Ten. I remember the look of him as if it was yesterday, walking toward me in his gold corduroy jacket, beige dress pants, and blue Adidas running shoes. He had asked me to dance at the very last opportunity, so I didn't go home from the high school dance without at least one turn around the gym. I was grateful, but it was a pained gratitude, like the gratitude of being the last one picked for the schoolyard team at recess, when you know no one really wants you to play.

If it was pity that got me a first invitation to tango, it was pleasure that got me a second. I learned that one of the greatest compliments you can give a tanguero is to leave him knowing he gave you pleasure. This need not be communicated with words. It's best communicated, quite simply, by enjoying yourself. This I did, thoroughly and unmistakably. My technique might have been flawed, my steps inconsistent, but there was never any doubt that I was delighted to be dancing. Cheek to cheek on the dance floor, he could feel me smile. Saying, "Thank you," as he walked me back to my seat was polite, but redundant.

These were the days when I danced in the liberty of incompetence. Of course, I gave every dance my best effort, but there was comfort in the knowledge that I was undeniably and very obviously a total beginner. For this brief time, I could dance step onto the dance floor without the burden of unrealistic expectations—my own or any one else's. Beginner's enthusiasm and starry-eyed awe carried me further than my limited experience would otherwise allow. I wore my love for tango on my sleeve, and what Jesus said about love covering a multitude of sins proved to be every bit as true on the dance floor as in the rest of life.

It didn't last.

The transition from novice to intermediate dancer is like another go at puberty. It's awkward, rife with insecurities and angst-ridden. I would like to say I was better at it the second time around. I was in my forties, after all, and had some experience to draw from. But, while I had slightly less acne and a better wardrobe this time around, it was still pretty awful.

Some nights, I could barely pretend to be satisfied to sit on the sidelines. Instead of basking in the beauty of the dance unfolding before me, I hosted a mean-spirited, juvenile debate in my head. "Who are you kidding? No one is going to dance with you. You're wasting your time!" taunted my inner-bully. "BUT I WANT TO DANCE!" cried my inner-whiner, stamping her little stilettos for effect. Sometimes, the bully won and I packed up my shoes with my hopes and went home early. Most of the time, my eagerness to dance kept me pinned to my chair, sometimes hoping so desperately for a dance that I trembled like a caffeinated Chihuahua. I would wait with all the angst of a schoolgirl with a devastatingly unrequited crush, giving up only when I heard the opening strains of La Cumparsita, the traditional final song of every milonga.

Worse, there were nights when I *did* get asked to dance and made such a muddle of it I had wished I had never set foot on the dance floor. I knew what I was supposed to do. I knew what I was supposed to look like. I knew what it was supposed to feel like. Watching me on the dance floor was living proof that a little knowledge is a dangerous thing. Gone was the happy liberty of incompetence. In its place was the crooked paralysis of expectation. Sometimes I thought so hard about what I was doing, even a basic left-right-left-right walking pattern felt like an impossibly complicated choreography. I might just as well have been trying to blow bubbles with my teeth wired together.

I was not alone in my misery. One night, shortly after I had been rescued from by ever-patient, breathe-with-me William (who stepped in when my less-patient and ill-mannered partner broke our embrace and started yelling instructions at me in the middle of the dance floor), I made friends with a young brunette who had plunked herself down in the chair next to me, sighed, and declared, "That was so awful, I feel like slitting my wrists." It was like being in Grade Eight again and feeling a special kinship with the only other girl in gym class who still hadn't gotten a bra.

I made other friends among the women on the sidelines, though it took a while. The dynamic between women in the tango community was different from any other I had experienced. The hybrid mix of camaraderie and competition took some getting used to. On the one hand, we were all in it together, sisters with a common desire for a lovely night of tango. On the other, there were a lot of women who would have preferred if everyone else on the sidelines had stayed home. Sometimes I saw it written on their faces as plainly as neon in a night sky, "Oh God, not another one! And a blonde, no less."

It also took a while to get used to the way conversations could stop abruptly and without warning. One minute I could be talking animatedly with my new best friend, and in a split second—which is all the time it takes for a *cabeceo* to travel back and forth across the dance floor—I would be sitting all by myself with an incomplete sentence hanging out of my mouth. If the conversation were between several women, the effect was more dramatic. The whole energy of the group would shift at the approach of a smiling tanguero.

If no *cabeceo* had been exchanged, this could be anyone's dance. Conversation would lag, someone might preen, sit up a bit taller, or smile coyly in the direction of the approaching stranger. Then, after the smiling tanguero had taken his chosen partner onto the dance floor, everyone would pick up the conversation where it had faltered, pretend to be okay with being left behind, and hope another tanguero might wander by the table. Soon.

I also learned that milongas, like any playground, have their bullies. I will never forget the cattiness I witnessed the night an unsuspecting ballroom dancer showed up in a salsa outfit worthy of a Las Vegas floorshow, dripping with ruffles and sequins. She seemed to be having a great time attempting tango for the first time, but this was no thanks to the self-appointed style police who wouldn't give her the time of day. And heaven help you if you get asked to dance "only" because you're beautiful. There's a pecking order on the sidelines, and—even though it would make far more sense to take it out on those men who favour beauty over skill—if you have the misfortune of being popular on the dance floor without first proving your skill as a dancer, brace yourself for scorn. This is no quilting bee.

At the same time, the women of the tango community did look out for each other, sharing information with each other in the interest of preventing injury. At first, since I had no reference points for this new community, I put this information in the same category as idle gossip. When I heard stories of bad behaviour among our local tangueros, I resolved to extend the benefit of the doubt and wait to form my own opinion. That's why, when the man they called The Back-Breaker asked me to dance, I agreed. Which is, in turn, why I had to stay home to ice my back the next day. On another occasion, I overheard a cautionary tale about a fellow who bragged that he'd taught himself how to tango by watching videos on the internet. I knew that I had met YouTube Guy a few nights later when he managed to kick me three times in our first turn around the dance floor. "What were you doing over there?" he asked after the first assault. "Don't you know that move?" he asked disdainfully after the second. "Why didn't you spread your legs?" he asked after the third. I was speechless in the face of his imagined prowess. In this way, my sisters on the sidelines earned credibility.

There was one other piece of advice circulated on the sidelines: "Never date a tanguero. There is no guarantee that the way he treats you on the dance floor will bear any resemblance to how he'd treat you on a date, let alone in a relationship." I heard detailed and extensive evidence on this point. So detailed and so extensive was the evidence, it became clear to me that this was a piece of advice very few heeded. The unspoken message was, "Wouldn't it be wonderful if your perfect partner on the dance floor was also your perfect life partner?" Which brought me right back to seeing the whole thing as another variation of high school, complete with schoolgirl angst over unrequited love.

Sometimes it was all a bit much. Often my head was spinning just as crazily on the sidelines as it was on the dance floor. I would periodically cloister myself in one of the pink metal toilet stalls of the women's bathroom to talk myself down from the edge. *Remember when it was okay to just watch, Sandra? Do that. Just watch. Let that be enough. Listen to the music, not the chatter. Listen for the beauty. Let that be enough.* Then I would take a deep breath, flush the empty toilet bowl, and head back to the hall to brave the sidelines once again.

I met Claude on a night like this. Claude and his wife, Hazel, were the hosts of the Tuesday night milonga and senior members of the local Argentine Tango community. As befit his role and stature in the community, Claude welcomed newcomers graciously and I was no exception. Sitting next to him—at his usual table at the northwest corner of the ballroom, near the stage—was a balm to my soul, the antidote for my wallflower anxiety. He was born and raised in France and was happy to indulge my desire to converse in French from time to time, adding another level of comfort to our interaction.

I learned that Claude's father, Genaro Espósito, was a respected tango composer, bandoneonist, and the leader of his own tango orchestra, *El Tano Genaro*. Genaro's career spanned continents, taking him from his home in Buenos Aires to the music halls of France. Listening to Claude's stories and watching him dance inspired me to a very particular sort of reverence: for his blood connection to a beloved composer from tango's Golden Age, for the way this music had accompanied him through the whole of his life—a tango soundtrack for everything from his earliest childhood memories through the loves and losses of a life now in its own golden age. I kept this awe to myself, of course. He would have brushed it off with a shake of his hands, a slight roll of his eyes, and a humble, polite smile, I suppose, but I didn't want to risk embarrassing him, or me and my romantic notions, for that matter.

There were nights that Claude also spent more time on the sidelines than on the dance floor. In his case this was because of roving aches and pains that afflicted him in spite of his best efforts to defy the encroaching limits of aging. It took me by surprise therefore when, one night after we'd lapsed gently into silence for several minutes, he asked me to dance. My palms began to sweat immediately, but there was no way I would give in to nerves and miss the opportunity to dance with my tango hero.

I entered his embrace tentatively, partly owing to nerves, partly owing to the fear that I might cause him pain. Though it may have had the appearance of a proper embrace, our frame had no substance. I held my body tightly to the bone, as far away from my skin as possible. This, of course, was awkward, uncomfortable, and entirely useless. I had accepted his invitation to dance and then offered him a cardboard cutout version of myself as a partner. I forced myself to trust him with my body, still careful to maintain balance over my own centre of gravity but daring to give myself more fully to the embrace. I may have imagined it, but at this moment I thought I heard Claude utter a sigh of relief.

We'd barely traversed half the ballroom when he spoke. "Hold your head still."

"Pardon me?" I wasn't sure I had understood, and hadn't expected him to speak.

"Hold your head still. When you look to the left and right and move your head around like that, it throws your balance. Your head is the heaviest part of you. It must be still."

I was proving myself to be the beginner I was, dancing first like a cardboard cutout and now like a dashboard bobble head. The error easy to correct and the effect was immediate. With my head next to his, no longer scanning for obstacles in the form of oncoming dancers, I had to trust him that much more, getting just that much closer to the surrender I had miraculously experienced with The Russian, once upon a time. It was a studied and partial surrender, but our connection improved all the same.

The final chords of the first song faded, we stepped out of the embrace. A lively thrum of conversation rose from the dancers on the floor, but between Claude and me there was silence. He stood opposite me with a deeply thoughtful look on his face. It was the look of someone measuring his words before speaking. Though things had improved over the course of the first song, our dance together was hardly poetry in motion. The music of the next song began and Claude still stood before me. I waited.

He broke the silence with a gesture. He reached out and placed his left hand on my right hip. This was clearly not an invitation to embrace. "The movement begins here," he said, staring at the place where he held my hip, to underline the point. "Here." I had learned in the studio that it was necessary to drop the hip for a proper extension of the leg in a back step. I had practiced the motion in my kitchen and in the grocery store checkout line. But here, with his hand on my hip, something clicked. What I knew and what I had practiced became something I could understand viscerally, with my body and my brain. Suddenly, I could comprehend the unbroken connection between the thought "step back" and the physical action of my hip and leg. Suddenly, there was no space between the impulse to move and the movement.

For all its apparent intimacy, the act of Claude putting his hand on my hip did not register as personal. It was technical. It was a practical, physical gesture, an act of instruction. Its effect was deep, visceral even, but practical. So it seemed at the time. Remembering that moment now, I can still feel the warmth and weight of his hand on my hip, like the hand of a potter on warm, malleable clay.

There was another embrace. And another. We danced the whole of the tanda. I kept my head still, as much out of a desire to heed Claude's instruction as the natural outcome of intensely focused thought. In the forefront of my mind was the memory of Claude's hand upon my hip. With each step I pictured the energy and the movement coming from precisely the place he touched, imagining the warmth and pressure of his hand to pinpoint the spot, picturing my hip in the form of an x-ray, and watching the hip joint move in the socket, just so. (Thinking back on it now, I wonder if in fact he did repeatedly place his hand upon my hip as we danced, so vivid is the memory of that sensation.) I marveled at how deeply right it felt when the thought matched perfectly with the sensation. I cringed when it did not. I imagined that Claude could sense exactly which steps came from the propulsive action of the perfect integration of mind and body, and which did not. It pleased me to imagine that he, too, took pleasure in the steps that reflected his instruction and the intentions of his touch upon my hip.

Here was a taste, again, of tango's sweetness. Unlike the Hallowe'en dance with The Russian, I did not lose myself in the experience of it. I returned to my seat on the sidelines not feeling disoriented or intoxicated, but simply and deliciously aware of having danced well. If not well, certainly better, and better because of Claude's gentle and clear direction. Clarity seems the best word for it. Clear and bright and true connections had been formed, my body had been freshly aligned. Something beautiful had broken through the chatter, the way a single bird's voice stands out from the rest once you've learned the bird and its song by name.

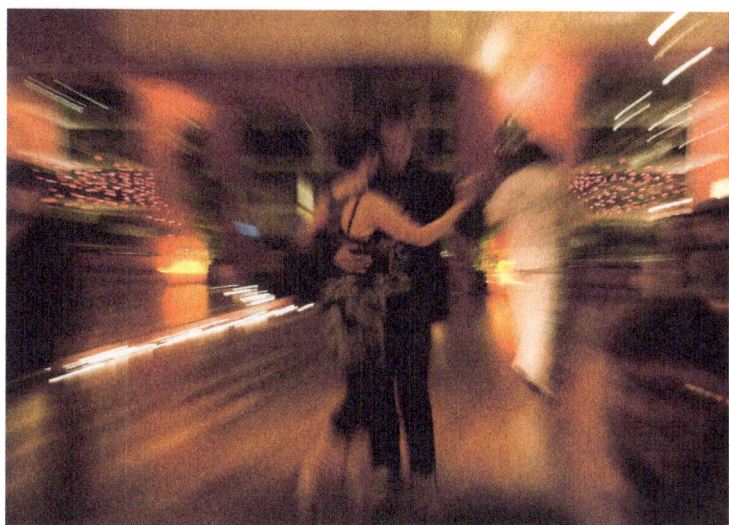

I have, on occasion, remembered things I have never experienced. At a dinner party not long ago, I told the story of a very special meal I once enjoyed at a little out-of-the-way tapas bar in Barcelona. I was halfway through the story before I remembered that I've never been to Spain. I was telling my friend Joanna's story—one she'd described so vividly that my salivating imagination had inadvertently slotted it in with memories of other delightful meals—meals I had actually consumed, in places I had actually visited. This is the power of story.

I heard Joanna's tapas story once and it got under my skin. I've heard Eve's story a thousand times or more—her story is in my bones. It is a story of beginnings and gardens and holiness, and about how everything went terribly, terribly wrong. I have never been to Eden, yet this storied garden is as real to me as any I've sown, weeded or watered. Eve and I have the same dirt under our fingernails; we sweat, we bleed, we remember, we long for better days.

I did not expect to hear anything new in the telling of the tale when it came up again in the church's rhythm of scripture readings on an otherwise ordinary Sunday morning, but I had never heard the story in such close proximity to a night of tango, with the sensation of tango's embrace still clinging to my skin—a visceral memory of intimacy and connection. "A reading from the book of Genesis," the reader begins. I hear the same words I've heard a thousand times before, but these words stand out: "And they were naked...and not ashamed." Naked, vulnerable, delighting in each other, reveling in the goodness of maleness and femaleness. The story continues with a choice, a thought, a gesture, and a decision—to set their own boundaries, to define their own freedom, to exchange God's design for a do-it-yourself version of life—and the curtain drops, like the cortina that breaks the spell of the tango's embrace. It's over. It's time to hide again behind masks of our own design.

"And the LORD called out to them, 'Where are you?' And they replied, 'We heard your voice in the garden and were afraid because we were naked, and we hid ourselves.'" I am sitting in the back row of the choir stalls and fully dressed, but it is to me that God poses the next question, "Who told you that you were naked?"

I did not hear the rest of the reading, or the sermon that followed. What I heard was this: When did you learn to be ashamed of who you are? Who taught you that you are less than who I made you to be? Why did you leave behind the delight of co-being with me and with the one I made to be your com-

panion? Don't turn your back on the Garden. Remember who you are.

Some months later, I heard someone describe tango as "a dance of nostalgia for a time we've never known," and I thought of Eden and the time when I was naked and not ashamed.

CHAPTER TEN

I became a regular at the Wednesday night practica at the EDAM Dance Studio, a rough-hewn gem of a studio hidden within the maze formed by the city street grid and two major thoroughfares. It always felt hectic to get there; it always felt good to arrive. Sometimes I arranged ahead of time for a partner for the night, sometimes I booked an instructor for a private lesson, but more often I just showed up. When there weren't enough leads to go around, or when I just wanted to get back to basics, I practised by myself on a little patch of floor in the far corner. I savoured these moments alone, though I suspect others pitied me for being without a partner. It gave me pleasure to take some time on my own, to reinforce what I was learning elsewhere without distraction.

In my Sunday evening class, Talia was pushing us to develop core strength and a keen kinesthetic awareness of the axis of our bodies. "Imagine a thread," she said, "Strung through every vertebra of your spine, through your neck, up through your head, straight up." She walked on tip toes as she spoke, her right arm raised above her head, tugging an invisible thread like a marionette pulling her own master wire. "You must maintain your axis at all times. Without it, the tango is impossible. At all times, one leg bears your weight and the other must be free, relaxed, ready to respond to your partner's lead." She stopped walking to demonstrate, standing tall and strong on her left leg, dropping her right hip, and languidly swinging her right leg in the air. Her torso was stable in spite of the lopsided action of her leg. "You must be strong here!" she said sharply, abruptly clapping her hands on her hips. "And here!" she said, clapping one hand over her belly and the other over her chest. "And also the pelvic floor," she added, feeling no need to point out its location, "It has to pull—together and up—along your axis."

On this particular Wednesday night, having practised for a few minutes with a tanguero friend whose girlfriend sulked noticeably the whole time, I happily took to the far corner of the studio to work alone. I walked a while, and then dedicated myself to standing axis exercises. *Weight on the left. Right leg free. Extend front, extend side, extend back... Extend front, extend side, extend back...* And so on, shifting my weight from one leg to the other when my muscles pleaded for a break. When both legs were begging for mercy, I switched to upper body rotation exercises.

With Talia's voice in my head, I planted my feet firmly—*Don't lock your knees, Sandra!*—held my arms before me like a ballerina in first position, and began. *Imagine a thread. Now, turning to the left, imagine your torso t-w-i-s-t-i-n-g around that thread, like a corkscrew. Start with the shoulders, hold your chest and abs in place. S-t-r-e-t-c-h. When you can hold back no longer, allow your chest to follow. S-t-r-*

e-t-c-h. Good. Now, let your abs follow. S-t-r-e-t-c-h. Now, back. Abs first—keep your chest and shoulders turned. P-u-l-l. Now, slowly, slowly, your chest comes back. Good. Now, your shoulders. And b-r-e-a-t-h-e. Good. Now turning to the right...

Talia had drilled this exercise into me out of necessity. In the beginning, I tended to turn from one side to the other with all the mindfulness of a casual shoulder check. To achieve the fluid movement of tango, I needed to learn how to dissociate my upper and lower body—to ensure that my shoulders and chest would maintain the frame of the embrace while my hips moved in a fluid rotation around my axis. Like the irritating but effective trick of remembering the name of the person you've just been introduced to at a dinner party—"So, Bob, how long have you lived in Vancouver, Bob?"—I dedicated myself to repetitive rotation exercises to gain a more precise familiarity with my own body parts.

With eyes closed, I visualized my torso as a reluctant corkscrew, twisting slowly and carefully along its curved prong. I pictured each separate muscle group and consciously called on one, and then the next, and then the next—each one pulling me further and further into the bend of my body and back again. *Shoulders, chest, abdomen, reverse. Abdomen, chest, shoulders, reverse. Shoulders, chest, abdomen, reverse.* At my centre, the thread of my axis pulled up, and up, and up—like a tight string of twine around which my muscles could wind and unwind. After a time, my inner voice no longer needed to call for muscles in turn, and I moved in and out of the curving by the silent voice of muscle memory. And then, I opened my eyes.

Natalie Goldberg once wrote, "If you turn around fast enough you might catch a glimpse of your true face," and I know that she is right. For there, in the mirrors of the far corner of the EDAM Dance Studio, I saw more than my reflection. As I curled my body from side to side in a seamless arc, with ballerina poise and bright eyes, I caught a glimpse of someone I once knew. Out of the corner of my eye, I saw a young girl, dancing in the night sky.

In the home my parents built when I was eleven years old, there was a Living Room of the capital letter variety. It was, together with the adjoining Dining Room, reserved for special occasions and, therefore, rarely used. The rooms were closed off from the rest of the house by sliding pocket doors, to keep out the smells of cooking and cigarette smoke, and to save on heating costs. The baseboard heaters smelled of dust and silence when they were turned on, one hour before the arrival of Company and not a moment earlier.

The rooms were sparsely furnished. My mother put huge houseplants in every corner to make the space feel smaller, hoping it gave the impression that the room was adequately furnished. An elegant cherry-wood buffet stood against the wall of the dining room, adorned with a crystal bowl, a dried flower arrangement and three family heirlooms—a gold-topped antique perfume bottle, a silver-clasped hymnbook, and a silver bud vase. In the centre of the room stood the cherry-wood dining table and six chairs upholstered in ivory brocade. There was a crystal chandelier over the table. It was a cheap imitation of a baroque-style chandelier but I didn't know the difference between crystal and glass and assumed the crystals were real. The adjoining living room was furnished with a coffee table, two end tables, a single armchair and a couch. The couch and armchair were of a set, French Provincial, with gold and olive green upholstery that showed no signs of wear, though the sun had faded the fabric in places. One of my household chores was dusting and I loved dusting these rooms most of all. I took special care with the perfume bottle whose soft gold cap bore the dimpled marks of teething ancestors.

To the north, the rooms looked over an expanse of lawn and the two small trees we'd planted after the bulldozers left—an English Oak and a Crimson King Maple. The real view was to the south: my beloved St. Lawrence River. I had lived in three houses up to that point in my life—all of them within a stone's throw of the river. To this day, I need a view of water to feel at home. This view was framed by a broad bay window with five parallel panes.

The first winter we lived in this house—when the days had become impossibly short and the nights impossibly long—I often took refuge in the cool apartness of these rooms. When I was safely assumed to be doing homework or getting ready for bed, I would quietly enter, turn up the dimmer switch just far enough for the golden glow of the chandelier to fill the centre of the room but not reach its corners. Against the pitch black of the winter sky, the five panes of the bay window were magically transformed into mirrors. When I danced in the golden light, five perfectly parallel reflections of me were magically transported into the night sky. I imagined myself gliding gracefully over the dark waters of my river, and my heart nearly burst for the joy of it.

At a time when the decidedly unenchanted mirrors of the world pointed at me with accusing fingers—at my acne, blotchy freckles, and the highly unexpected downy hairs that had recently appeared on my upper lip—the windows of my nighttime sanctuary reflected a prettier me. Here, I could still look at myself with kind eyes. Accompanied by the music of my imagination, I danced unselfconsciously—spinning on mountain tops with Maria von Trapp, imitating the pliés and pirouettes of The Nutcracker's Sugarplum Fairy, and creating my own wildly uncoordinated choreographies for the sheer pleasure of it.

The accusing fingers of household mirrors were not the only judges I lived with in the world beyond the cocoon of those sliding pocket doors. I was subjected—like everyone else—to the pointed admonishments of a consumer culture hell bent on convincing me that my body was flawed and embarrassing and desperately in need of just the right product to remedy the situation. And, much closer to home—under the same roof, in fact—I lived with another accuser. I lived with a constant, hateful, jabbing insistence that I was fat, and ugly, clumsy, and inadequate in every possible way. I lived with an older brother who despised me. We get along well enough now, and I joke that as the first born, he just took a really long time to get over the shock of having to share the world with a baby sister, but I still carry scars and the scars run deep. After years of therapy, years of forgiving, I regret that it's still hard to forget.

It's hard to forget the hours I spent in the fragile refuge of the upstairs bathroom. It was the only room in the house with both a lock and a drawer that could be pulled open to bar the way if the lock failed. There are deep cracks on both sides of the lacquered finish of that door, testifying to the rage that hammered, and hammered, and hammered against it. I don't know why my parents never noticed those cracks—or, for that matter, the cracked spindle on the upstairs baluster. I remember the sharp pinch of broken wood against the skin of my back when it broke, having fallen hard against the rail after a particularly rough shove. My brother straightened the spindle so the fracture looked more or less like a manufacturer's flaw. It's a wonder no one ever tested its strength.

Nor can I forget the hours I spent lying in my bed, trembling with adrenaline. My brother had the erratic habit of opening my bedroom door, turning on the lights, and slamming the door shut again. He didn't do it every night. He didn't always do it at the same time. Sometimes I was sound asleep, sometimes I was dozing off, sometimes I would have only just turned off my bedside lamp. Always, it sent a charge of adrenaline through my body, knotted my stomach, and, eventually, forced me out of bed to turn off the light again. This I did in fear, worrying that the light switch trick might be a ploy to get me near the door so that he could grab me and hurt me without much effort. For a long time, I had nightmares of dark, menacing figures standing over my bed.

The door to my room seemed to belong to him more than to me. One Sunday afternoon, I was changing out of my church clothes after Sunday dinner. An uncle and aunt were visiting with their four boys. The boys had been holed up in my brother's bedroom, amusing themselves with an old television that had conveniently broken in just the manner necessary to serve as an impromptu strobe light. With my brother's uncanny sense of timing, just as I stood naked but for my underwear, they burst into my room. I lunged for the door, but couldn't close it against the force of five boys. The best I could do was cower behind the door, huddled in the narrow wedge formed by the door and the wall, holding the door knob with white knuckles with one hand, and trying to cover my adolescent breasts with the other.

Remembering all this, I am startled and somewhat awed by the courage and optimism of the young girl I once was—the young girl who tiptoed into the winter cold of the living room to secretly dance in a bit of golden light. I do not know how I managed to suspend my awareness that the only thing standing between me and the rest of the world were two sliding pocket doors.

On one occasion, my mother startled me by abruptly opening the door to the kitchen, having sensed—as mothers do—that something was up. "What's going on in there? It's too cold for you here. Come set the table for supper." I felt foolish, caught doing something I was sure my mother would consider frivolous and childish. On another occasion, my brother—by whatever sense brothers have—knew something was up, and stealthily slid open the hallway door, the door furthest from earshot.

He spied on me for a while before bursting in. He circled around me in a crude, violent imitation of the dance he'd witnessed. Five taunting reflections writhed around me in the night sky. "Porky thinks she can dance!" He jabbed at me with hard fingers, making pig noises and laughing.

It was some time before I returned to my secret studio again, but return I did. And again, without warning, my brother also returned. By then the magic was thin, diluted by fear, and there was little joy in the golden light of the bay window. There was no third time. I can almost feel the cold plastic of the dimmer switch as I turned it slowly back, until the golden light of the chandelier was extinguished, and with it five perfectly parallel reflections of a young girl being slowly cut off from herself.

Five thousand kilometers and thirty years away, I stood before the mirrors of the Edam Dance Studio, turning from side to side, taking deep rhythmic breaths. Sweat dripped from my brow and upper lip, and trickled down the backs of my legs in long, thin rivers. My muscles burned in long strong lines; tendons and ligaments pulled and released, pulled and released. I delighted in the arc I carved into space with the full moon circle of my arms, steady and round and strong. *Imagine a thread, strung through every vertebra of your spine... Up and up and up and up...* And I felt my soul reaching along that thread, with an ache and a longing and bittersweet joy. I was dancing in the night sky again, dancing high above the river's dark waters. It felt like coming home.

I am kneeling at the altar rail, shoulder to shoulder with the twenty other folks who managed to come to church on a rainy Wednesday afternoon. I catch a waft of perfume from the elderly woman kneeling next to me. Lily of the Valley, I think, like the Avon perfume my mother kept on her dresser but never wore. It smells like spring.

My priest dips his thumb into an earthen bowl of ash, and looks me in the eye. "Remember that you are dust and to dust you shall return." He presses his thumb onto my forehead in two quick gestures, leaving behind two smudged lines of ash in the shape of a cross. "Remember that you are dust and to dust you shall return," he says to Lily of the Valley, and to the woman next to her, and so on, shuffling sideways along the altar rail, crisscrossing our faces with ash and reminding each of us in turn that we are dust.

The ashes are made of last year's Alleluias, the black dust remains of the palm fronds and songs we lifted up on Palm Sunday—the now distant day that had overflowed with hope for a world beyond sorrow, beyond pain, beyond tears. Our greatest hopes and best intentions lie burnt and crushed in a small earthen bowl. Chrism oil has been stirred into the ash—the sacred oil used in baptism to mark the foreheads of those chosen by God, holy and beloved. It makes the ashes dark, fragrant, and sticky. "Remember you are dust and to dust you shall return." Remember you are broken. Remember you are holy. Remember the mystery of your faith.

It is Ash Wednesday, the first day of Lent. This is our season of remembering, our season of repentance and reconciliation, forty days to turn away from that which robs us of our holiness, forty days to remember that God does amazing things with dust. I get up from my knees and step away from the altar rail with the rest of this tiny congregation, resisting the urge to wipe my forehead where it tickles under the sticky ash. We return back to our pews, gather our belongings, and step out into the world again, wearing ragged hope and holiness on our skin for everyone to see.

CHAPTER ELEVEN

Time does strange things in the world of tango. I was still working long hours and keeping up with responsibilities beyond work, yet I always had time for another class or milonga. Time seemed to magically expand beyond the limits of twenty-four hours to the day to allow me more and more time for dancing. It was as if I had found a portal into a parallel universe where time stood still. Hours spent at a milonga did not pass in the same predictable, measurable manner of hours spent anywhere else. In the arms of the right tanguero, time fell away, lost all conventional meaning. In spite of the fact that the music we were dancing to was as bound by time as the hands of a clock, there was a timeless stillness within the embrace, one that transcended the mundane passage of one minute into the next.

I've never been a huge fan of fantasy or science fiction, but pondering the mystery of tango time sent my mind in unexpected directions. What if, by drawing together all that is tragic and all that is delightful in love and life, tango creates such a perfect balance that a timeless space is created between them? What if, in combination with precisely the right level of hunger for beauty, tango musicians and dancers happened upon the exact combination of music and movement to break the code for time travel, making it possible to spend the evening in the tango salons of Buenos Aires without ever leaving Vancouver? But my thoughts came back to earth, and with it the realization that what I was experiencing here was better than any flight of fancy. I did not need time travel or magical interruptions in the time-space continuum. I just needed to get myself to the Polish Community Centre or whatever venue was hosting a milonga that night, and I needed to dance.

Dancing became almost a substitute for sleep for me, a pastime nearly as refreshing and necessary as time spent under the covers. Of course, there were times when I was brutally fatigued, but somehow it didn't matter. It was different from run-of-the-mill tiredness, the kind that makes you long for twelve uninterrupted hours of sleep. Instead of craving more sleep, I craved more tango. When the rest of the city brushed, flossed and put on pajamas, I brushed, flossed, put on my little black dress, and headed out for the nearest milonga. It felt like lost years were being restored to me there on the dance floors of Vancouver, as if time had been plucked out of the black hole of depression and given back to me for the sole purpose of dancing.

I danced with my kite-flying friend who also ended up taking lessons and whose progress—from early joys to later frustrations—paralleled my own. He'd taken up classical ballet in his early twenties (on a dare), added contact improvisation in his thirties, and figured that tango would round things out nicely in his forties. He loved to remind me "the floor is your first dance partner" and would sometimes break our embrace to whip off a couple of pirouettes if he was getting frustrated with himself. His steps were BIG, his gestures dramatic, and his enthusiasm contagious. He was also tall, and I would sometimes seek him out after I had danced with someone shorter than me; most of the time height doesn't matter much, but there were times I left the dance floor feeling like an awkward Amazonian, and a tanda in his arms was the perfect antidote.

I got to be a favourite of a handsome Moroccan who'd come to the city for a few months on a research project. He was as passionate about soccer ("football") as tango and sometimes seemed to forget the difference between the two. We arranged to meet at the Wednesday night practica a couple of times. Both times I left at the end of the night feeling as if we had spent the hours doing skills-and-drills instead of tango. But the night he came to the Saturday milonga at Yasel's, wearing his best suit and new tango shoes—the night I wore my green halter dress for the first time, with my hair drawn up into a French knot, and with rhinestone earrings to catch the light—he did not for a minute forget that we were there to dance and his embrace was tender and strong and gentle.

But there was no need to make a fuss over visiting tangueros. I was in very good company with the dancers who called Vancouver home, and as I got to know them over the next months—and they got to know me—I came to appreciate each of them for the particular qualities they brought to the embrace and to the dance. I always looked forward to a vals with Paulo—the man one friend referred to as the *Mercedes Benz* of tangueros, "Always elegant, smooth, and with an embrace that fits just so." And Guillermo, whose lead was perhaps less refined than Bernardo's but who always took such exquisite care of his follows—never neglecting the gentlemanly tradition of walking me back to my seat after a dance, and generous with compliments. "Qué linda!" he'd say, "So beautiful!" I ate it up. And Anil, who gave himself to the dance so fully I could not help but be drawn into the same story. Like the needle on a compass finding true North, I would find myself effortlessly aligned with his body as we danced. He never pushed me beyond my ability, but in his arms I always felt more accomplished than my experience merited. He was the very model of the tanguero who takes upon himself the duty to make his partner look and feel exquisite on the dance floor.

These were the men whose respect for tango etiquette earned my trust. It was within this trust that tango bestowed a gift beyond any trick of time. Within the carefully maintained boundaries of tango's embrace, I learned what it was like to be a woman and feel safe at the same time. It felt like a miracle. Here, I did not have to be anything less than the woman I was—not guarded out of fear that I would be a target for oppression or violence, nor rendered asexual out of a fear of being seen as a temptress. I learned how not to fear men or the feelings that arose in me in their arms.

When, during a particularly sensual tango, Marco's fingers accidentally grazed my neck as he adjusted his embrace, it sent an electric shock through my body and for a moment I felt both aroused and afraid. But we just kept dancing. I quickly realized that there was no intention of control or seduction in his touch, no manipulation of emotion or power. We were telling a story together with the language of the body; it was a powerful, sensual story being told in words of touch and movement that were equally powerful and sensual. There was no question that the intimacy of the embrace remained on the dance floor, no overstepping the bounds of the *cortina* which—like the curtain it is named for—separates the time shared as partners from the time shared as friends, with a gentle but distinct barrier.

Once, after a beautiful set of three songs, the man I had been dancing with launched into comments that started with, "Oooh, was that ever HOT!" and ended with, "Wanna go out for a drink later?" On this occasion, I did not appreciate being walked back to my place on the sidelines. It did not feel like the courtesy it was supposed to be; it felt rather more like being stalked. But apart from having to politely reject drink invitations for the next several weeks, there were no lasting complications. In a tango community as small as Vancouver's there's an automatic check on unwelcome behaviour.

I did not always manage to keep my own emotions within the gentle bounds of the musical cortinas. I developed a crush on a local tanguero with a reputation for playing the field, in large part because of how beautifully he danced, and in small part because I have a horrible weakness for foreign accents and broad shoulders and he had both. I kept my eye on him in spite of the vast numbers of very red flags waving around him, ignoring obvious warnings in favour of giving him "the benefit of the doubt." I even managed to ignore the warning flags he waved himself—like the time he told me, as a statement of fact, that he could sense immediately upon entering a venue which women he could sleep with that night if he chose to; or the time he said, point blank, that he was an asshole and dating him would be a mistake. When I told one of my closest friends that, she threw up her arms in exasperation and shouted, "For God's sake, San! It's *unanimous! I* know he's bad for you. *You* know he's bad for you. *He* knows he's bad for you. *Enough!*" For several weeks I was caught in the embarrassing high school cliché of good-girl-wants-bad-boy. I didn't manage to shake the crush until his bad boy ways were made so boldy and personally manifest that I came to my senses quite suddenly and that was the end of that.

That was the end of that until the Frenchman came to town, that is. He was classically French—tall, dark, and handsome—with a lovely accent and playful milonguero style on the dance floor. He was a brilliant conversationalist; we could spend hours talking about almost anything. I had even gone so far as to give him lodging while he looked for a job and an apartment of his own. But there were red flags flying around his tall, dark, handsome French-ness, and this time it didn't take me so long to take heed.

Things came to something of a dramatic end with the Frenchman after a fateful milonga we attended together, where he ignored not only me but every other woman in the hall in favour of one endless embrace with a starry-eyed blonde. This was personally insulting on two levels: not only had my date ditched me publicly, he had marked me as a bad judge of character insofar as I had come to the milonga with a man who had little regard for the rules of tango etiquette—specifically, the rule that prohibits back-to-back tandas with the same partner. With back-to-back-to-back tandas for more than two hours, there was no further need for red flags. I surprised myself by leaving him to his captive audience and heading home by myself. This wasn't mean in and of itself—after all, he didn't even notice I had gone until the milonga ended. What was mean was that I knew he didn't have a key to get in on his own, I turned the ringer off to the entry phone, and wore earplugs to bed for good measure. He may have been arrogant, and self-serving, and disrespectful of tango etiquette, but I had broken every rule of hospitality in the book. What's more, though I should be ashamed to admit it, I was kind of proud of myself for I'd done. It was strangely satisfying to learn that he'd had to beg another tenant for entrance to the building and then had slept in the hall until I finally heard him knock at the door again around six in the morning. It was the meanest thing I had ever done.

I found my way back to the tangueros who'd taught me not only how to dance, but how to respect myself, in and out of the embrace. On the first Tuesday night after the debacle with the Frenchman, I was moved to tears while dancing with a tender-hearted friend. He danced me to the hall entrance, led me out to the lobby, and sat with me there until there were no more tears. Then he stood up, extended his hand, and led me back to the dance floor to finish what we'd begun. After every disappointment, there was a tanguero ready to remind me how to trust myself to tango's embrace.

At a private lesson with Talia once, the man who'd come as my partner for the hour commented on how quickly I could embody the corrections Talia pointed out in my technique. "It's remarkable. She tells you what's wrong, and you stop doing it. Just like that! I've never seen anything like it." I hoped I could be as quick a study off the dance floor, throwing off my blinkers and trusting my judgment over the appeal of broad shoulders, foreign accents, and a tempting embrace.

CHAPTER TWELVE

I was not wearing blinders the week The German came to town. I did not find him particularly attractive, though he was well dressed, tall, and had a nice enough build. I don't even fancy German accents. I watched him dance in the early part of the evening and he seemed unlikely to fall into rank with The Back Breaker or YouTube Guy. When he glanced my way, I met his eyes. When he approached with his hand extended, I stood, walked with him to a gap in the line of dance, and accepted his offer of embrace. We fit well together, had an easy connection, and enjoyed a tanda of dances as much as anyone could hope to. He had an exceptional ear for the music and communicated his interpretation clearly and succinctly. It was easy to meet his *cabeceo* again later in the night, easy to step into his embrace with the same trust.

The music of our second tanda together began with the strong punch of the bandoneon. We waited. The strings entered. We found each other's breath, and waited. When the piano joined the music, he took his first step, inviting me into the space he'd created. We danced in close embrace. I knew exactly where we were going and how to parry his strength. It was electric. I felt eyes upon us as we danced and self-consciousness started to creep in. I did not want a preoccupied brain to hinder my dancing, so I tuned my focus more intensely on the music and the movements of my partner, until my mind gave itself over completely to the dance. The space between us was barely perceptible.

The first song of the tanda ended with a long and luxuriant phrase, which we traced in a long and luxuriant gesture—my leg extended, my foot gliding over the floor in a wide arc. Then, in perfect synchronicity with the final staccato chord of the bandoneon, my thigh contracted, pressed up against his tightened frame. I held my breath for a split second longer, to savour the perfect finish and to anticipate one of my favourite tango moments—the moment when you see your partner face to face for the first time since the dance began and smile at each other in the shared satisfaction of knowing you've made something beautiful together.

When I took a breath again, expecting in that moment to be released from the embrace—as was the case after every other song of every other tanda I had ever danced—he did not let me go. He held me there, in the imperceptibly small space of our embrace. I laughed uncomfortably, assuming it was some kind of joke, but his arms did not loosen. He started whispering—something about how beautiful I was, how beautiful Vancouver was, how he could make a life for himself here—and his breath felt hot against my skin. I couldn't see a way to get out of his embrace without making a scene.

Mercifully, the second song of the tanda began, and the embrace that had begun to feel like a trap was once again restored to its rightful purpose. It took more than one turn around the floor to shake the claustrophobic sensation of being trapped between floors in a broken elevator, but the power and beauty of his dance was so compelling, I gave myself over to it willingly and dismissed his earlier behaviour as a bad joke.

The strain of the violin's last note faded from hearing at the end of the second song and again he held me tight. I started to panic. Couples around us had separated and were chatting amiably. Again he whispered warm, wet words in my ear. I heard nothing but my pulse. My mind raced: *Don't make a scene, Sandra. Don't embarrass yourself. You stepped into his embrace willingly. You got yourself into this.* The music began again, but this time there was no relief in it. His embrace, unchanged, did not magically conform once again to its rightful purpose. He lead me around and around the dance floor but I did not dance. I had curled away from my skin and tucked myself into my brain to watch the scene from a distance. For all appearances, there was no difference in the quality of our dance between the first and last dance of the tanda. I could not understand my fear, nor quell it. I had agreed to another dance, but he'd taken more than a dance from me.

When a friend observed to me, moments later, "Wow! What incredible dancing! It's as if he sees right through you." I did not know how to reply. Yes, the dancing was incredible. The connection was powerful. And it shook me to the core, not with beauty but with fear. He saw right through me because I made myself invisible. I had absented myself entirely from the dance and no one noticed. Least of all him.

I mark myself with the sign of the cross as I enter the places where I dance. It is a simple gesture and it grounds me. I make the gesture with an open palm—ready to give, ready to receive—touching my index finger to my forehead, dropping my hand down to touch my diaphragm, then sweeping quickly from left to right across my chest, from shoulder to shoulder, and then resting, for just a moment, at the centre point of my chest. This reminds me who and whose I am.

I am drawing myself in this gesture, tracing my identity with invisible thread and five light touches: here, where my thoughts reside; here, the place of breath and hunger, heartbeat and longing; then here and here, remembering my reach and my embrace; and then here, pausing for a moment at the centre of me. I am not only the sum of my thoughts, nor am I a collection of body parts. I will think and feel and move and remember that I am whole, and all of me dances.

I mark myself as I have so often been marked by others, marked as God's own forever. This cross is the mark of my belonging. The God who breathes life into dust and ashes has called me beloved, has wept with me and held me, and, when the time was right, has taught me to dance. This is God's beloved

Sandra stepping over that threshold onto the dance floor. I am sacred space.

For a moment, the shape of a cross hangs in the air, suspended in the thin sliver of time and space—between me, standing on the threshold of a dance hall, and the promise of a night of tango. In this place, people will meet and embrace. In each embrace lies the possibility of wholeness or brokenness, the possibility of communion or loneliness, the possibility of beauty or pain. This is a meeting place for generosity, humility, strength, vulnerability, kindness, and respect. This is sacred space.

CHAPTER THIRTEEN

As the days lengthened and spring folded itself into summer, I reveled in my newfound passion. Improvements in my skill and ability came more slowly and were hard-earned, but I had cemented my place among the local intermediate dancers and was content there. Fully aware that I would have to walk many more miles in my *Comme Il Faut* stilettos to be considered an advanced dancer, I was learning how to dance in the becoming place—reaching ahead for more while savouring the present moment. Just as I cast off impromptu *boleos* in the checkout line and crosswalk, I pulled as much of the wholeness I experienced when I danced into the life I lived beyond the dance floor. I had crossed the threshold from *having* a body to *being* a body, and nothing—not depression, not insecurity-driven mental gymnastics, not perfectionism, not visiting Germans—was going to take that away from me. These were the enemies I could name; just around the corner was another one, about to be introduced.

It did not rattle me the second time I found mail from the BC Cancer Agency in my mailbox. I tucked it under my arm, along with the phone bill and the latest Vancouver Art Gallery flyer, and got in the elevator. I would read it after dinner. I was hungry and it could wait. The ultrasound tech-

nician that had done my follow-up ultrasound the year before—the ultrasound that determined the suspicious mass
was a false finding—had explained that because I have dense
breasts, this would likely not be the last time I had to deal
with a false-positive test result. When I read the letter and
saw the words, "suspicious mass" again, I groused a bit to myself over the fact that a follow-up ultrasound would be a nui-
sance to fit into my schedule, but I did not panic. Even when
I was called in to my family doctor's office a few days after the
ultrasound, I expected it was going to be a routine visit. "You
have cancer," were not the words I was expecting to hear.

A year earlier, the prospect of such a diagnosis had spun
me into a whirlwind of anxiety. Now, with the reality of the
diagnosis hanging in the air between me and my doctor, I
felt an unusual calm. She put a box of tissues within my
reach and began to explain what was going to happen next. In
spite of the fact that my world had just been turned upside-
down, everything she said made sense to me. I started taking
notes—appointment times, surgeon's name, oncologist's
name, radiation consult, studies—notes that I would later
transfer into what I called my "cancer book," a hardcover
journal with a Chinese painting of bamboo on the cover. I
chose the book for its cover. A small paragraph inside the cover told me that the artist's "lucid, firm, single brushstrokes
convey the nature and virtues of bamboo—resilience, humility and uprightness, the spirit that can be bent by circum-
stance but never broken." I understood this in a way I could

not have understood it a year earlier. Tango had given me a sense of my own resilience, a sense of the grace that surrounded and infused me, and an axis I could trust to keep me focused and strong.

I was scheduled for surgery on Wednesday, the sixteenth of July. There was no question in my mind that I would go dancing as usual on Tuesday night. There was no way to know how long it would be until I could dance again, no way to know how much of me would be left for dancing once the cancer was cut away, no way to know much of anything. I wore my hot pink dress in the hope that it would inspire me to dance boldly in the face of these countless unknowns—this was no night for black—but I did not dance particularly boldly. I danced truly. Though it was no truer this night than at any other point in my life, I had an especially acute awareness that I was standing on the thin, thin edge between wholeness and brokenness. I was so grateful to have learned that I could dance on that edge.

Only a few of my closest tango friends knew that I was scheduled for surgery the next day. I didn't want to be the breast cancer poster girl of the tango community, so I kept it pretty quiet. Word would get around soon enough. Those who knew were not surprised that I came out dancing on the eve of major surgery. We were all glad for music and the movement to fill the place of words when there was so much and so little to be said. I recall laughing when one tanguero told me, "You're you, you're strong, you're beautiful. Cancer can't beat you!" I asked him if he honestly believed beauty had anything to do with fighting cancer. He answered, "Yes!" and now I believe him. Not because I think physical appearance has any bearing on the success of eliminating cancer, but because by keeping my focus on beauty, I found the strength to endure the violence and pain of cancer treatments without losing hope.

I knew that making the shift from "I have a body" to "I am a body" had life-changing implications, but I had not anticipated what this would mean for when it came to cancer treatments. I resisted putting on the anonymous blue hospital gowns I was instructed to wear for examinations and radiation treatments, preferring to just remove my street clothes when nudity was required. I wanted my caregivers to know me as a woman whose wardrobe reflected her particular personality and taste. I memorized my Cancer Agency chart number for efficiency's sake, but made sure to introduce myself by name to every health professional that crossed my path, and I got their names, too. I knew perfectly well this was no cocktail party, but I was not going to spend half my life in waiting rooms, examination rooms and radiation chambers without knowing the names of the folks I was hanging out with.

I discovered that pain could do more than any German tanguero ever could to make me want to dissociate from my body. On the Thanksgiving weekend, an infection erupted in my surgery site, producing an abscess bigger than my already swollen breast. The emergency staff at the Cancer Agency had thrown several different antibiotics at it, but there was no change. The pain was excruciating, and it just got worse and worse. I was wheeled into an ultrasound examination room for a needle aspiration. I held onto the side rail of the gurney as if my life depended on it. The technician had to excuse himself twice: once to put on soothing music—bless his heart, but there was no convincing me this was a spa treatment—and a second time, I'm sure, to calm his nerves. I had not understood the phrase "wracked with pain" until this. When I had to have a semi-permanent drain installed the next day, I asked a doula friend to come to the clinic to hold my hand. She'd helped a thousand babies come into the world and with those same hands holding mine, I knew I could bear the pain and not lose sight of who I was.

In the midst of all the numbers—pathology reports, lab tests, chart entries, tumour margins, survival rates—I had friends to remind me that my life was overflowing with things that could not be numbered, things that cancer could never touch. One afternoon, my friends Joanna and Wade visited me with their then three-year old daughter, Sophia. I met them at their car and was nearly bowled over when Sophia burst out of her car seat and raced at me to cover my face with kisses. I knew her as an affectionate little girl, but this was an exceptionally exuberant display of affection. They told me later that when they'd told her that they were coming to see me and that I was "very, very sick," Sophia had asked if maybe they should just stay home so they wouldn't catch whatever it is I had. When they explained that cancer wasn't like a cold or runny nose and could, in fact, be made better with hugs and kisses, Sophia had taken things into her own hands.

When cancer treatments and ongoing complications had stretched my finances beyond expectations, my friends put together a fundraising event for me. The vulnerability I had felt in the week after my surgery when I had to have a girl-friend bathe me and wash my hair as I knelt in the bathtub was nothing compared to this. Hundreds of people were be-ing invited, people I didn't even know were making donations for a silent auction, there would be music, dancing, food, and wine—and not just any wine, but Joie Farms wine, to really kick cancer in the teeth. Accepting this gift required a level of humility I had never had to summon and I did not know if I had it in me. They called the fundraiser the "Truly Beauti-ful Night" and raised enough to cover my living expenses for nearly a year.

At only one point in this cancer experience did I almost lose sight of beauty: When the very drug meant to improve my chance of surviving cancer propelled me into a depression so deep I spent three days lying on the floor of my living room, weeping. I made an emergency appointment with my oncol-ogist and told her that I would rather die of cancer than live another day wishing I were dead. That was a price too high to pay.

It took several months to fully regain the use of my right arm after the infection. For months I did daily exercises designed to enhance blood flow, break down scar tissue, and build strength—all with a view to raising it to shoulder level again in tango's embrace. On my first night back at the Polish Community Centre, I danced only once. The rest of the night I received the love and welcome of my community, soaked in the music and watched the beauty unfold on the dance floor in front of me. And it was enough.

I will let these sparks flame. I have felt the benediction of water and the sustaining presence of wind. I have allowed myself to be shaped and I have shaped myself—again and again—out of dust and ashes. I will trust this fire. I will not be afraid.

CPSIA information can be obtained at www.ICGtesting.com
Printed in the USA
LVOW01s0149250913

353959LV00003B/5/P